ID0940492

WE GOT BY

LON HAMMONDS ON MAIN STREET

WE GOT BY

A BLACK FAMILY'S JOURNEY
IN THE HEARTLAND

RIC S. SHEFFIELD

TRILLIUM, AN IMPRINT OF
THE OHIO STATE UNIVERSITY PRESS
COLUMBUS

Copyright © 2022 by Ric S. Sheffield.
All rights reserved.
Trillium, an imprint of The Ohio State University Press.

Library of Congress Cataloging-in-Publication Data
Names: Sheffield, Ric S., 1954– author.
Title: We got by : a Black family's journey in the Heartland / Ric S. Sheffield.
Other titles: Black family's journey in the Heartland
Description: Columbus : Trillium, an imprint of The Ohio State University Press, [2022] |
    Includes bibliographical references. | Summary: "A Kenyon College professor relates
    his family's story in this memoir about the rural Ohio life of three generations of a
    Black family through the twentieth century"—Provided by publisher.
Identifiers: LCCN 2022013433 | ISBN 9780814258422 (paperback) | ISBN 9780814282298
    (ebook)
Subjects: LCSH: Sheffield, Ric S., 1954—Family. | Sheffield family. | Hammond family.
    | African Americans—Ohio—Genealogy. | African Americans—Ohio—Biography. |
    Mount Vernon (Ohio)—Biography. | Ohio—Genealogy. | African Americans—Social
    conditions—Ohio—20th century.
Classification: LCC E185.93.O2 S54 2022 | DDC 929.20973—dc23/eng/20220323
LC record available at https://lccn.loc.gov/2022013433

Cover design by adam bohannon
Text design by Juliet Williams
Type set in Adobe Caslon Pro

♾ The paper used in this publication meets the minimum requirements of the American
National Standard for Information Sciences—Permanence of Paper for Printed Library
Materials. ANSI Z39.48-1992.

*In loving memory of my grandmother,
Bertha Ruthanna Edwards Fisher Hammonds,
and my mother, Oneida Mae Fisher Sheffield
Lawson—the women who inspired us all and
whose spirits continue to watch over us.*

CONTENTS

ILLUSTRATIONS

PROLOGUE

At the time, it seemed important that I begin with pen in hand, pressing firmly onto the smooth, empty page. The thoughts that were swirling around in my head were so personal and emotional that it didn't seem right to sit at a keyboard having them disrupted by the mechanical clicking, my eyes chasing a cursor that mindlessly darted around the sterile screen. Delving deep into my family's past took more courage than I thought I had but knew that I would need. It wasn't just that there were bound to be skeletons like many families have lurking in their closets; it was coming face-to-face with the details about the long-unspoken tragedies that made me apprehensive. The people and events that this odyssey would involve necessarily included the dark and painful as well as the joyful and inspiring. Not only was I uncertain about how my relatives would receive the revelations about family secrets that ranged from heartless infidelity to violent deaths, I wasn't sure how well I would handle things like the emerging truth about a suicide and a wrongful conviction in my family, neither of which were ever mentioned or spoken about for more than sixty years. In fact, the latter has never been discussed and will likely become known to them and the rest of our small community for the first time in this writing.

I suspected that I already had more information about my family than many, if not most, of the other members. I also believed that as a consequence of the several interviews that I conducted and some meticulous research over the years that I had discovered stories and accessed historical documents that few others had seen or even knew existed. Locating and requesting military records, census reports, court documents, and birth certificates answered only some of the easier questions about dates and places. Reading newspaper accounts, long-lost letters, and diaries gave texture to the faces in the photographs that filled the shoeboxes lying dormant in family members' closets. Still, encountering long forgotten news articles, even if at one time available to the general public, confirmed what I had long suspected, or disclosed things about which I could never have imagined, and resulted in numerous sobering moments and more than an occasional tear.

Most of the time, I wasn't even sure why I had undertaken this project. I knew that there were people in my life over nearly seven decades that my children never had a chance to know. Of course, memories can be notoriously inaccurate, especially when the stories involve one's family. Yet, the old saying that "a man never really dies until he is no longer remembered" was one that seemed to ring true for me. Perhaps, it was my grandfather, Reverend Sam Sheffield, whose words about remembrance sunk most deeply into me that called me to take up what might become a perilous, emotional journey. My siblings and I traveled to tiny Martinsville, Virginia, in the foothills of the Blue Ridge Mountains, for one last visit with him as he lay dying at age ninety-two in the final stages of terminal cancer. I sat on a stool close by as my grandfather, a former coal miner who had late in life finally received the black lung benefits from the federal government that were due to him, spoke softly, the raspy air forcing itself through his lungs. His sad gray eyes looked into mine as he said, "Son, as long as you live, I will live. I will be remembered as long as you live." I took that to mean that it was my responsibility to make sure that my children and their children would know him through me. And if I did it well, then knowing him and all the others of our family would happen for many generations to come, perhaps throughout eternity. It would be impossible to share these people's lives and my attachment to them simply through discolored photo albums and cold lists or charts of names and dates.

From the outset, it was clear that I had to discover and rediscover stories that could bring to life for my children, and perhaps theirs someday, the many persons who defined for me what family was and helped to shape my understanding of what the world had been for generations of small-town "colored folks."

It wasn't enough to construct a meticulously researched family tree that memorialized our genealogical lineage. It was equally important to me that I try to convey how time, place, and cultural circumstance influenced how we saw ourselves in the context of the broader community. For more than a century and a half, many members of our large extended and mixed-race family lived in rural environments where we were often among only a handful of other persons of color. Sometimes, we were the only ones. That numerical absence with the resulting sense of isolation, even if and when deeply subconscious, affected our identities in ways that continue to be discernible many years later.

I use the labels "colored," "Black," "Negro," and "African American" when the people themselves would have more likely used these terms or their usage was more commonplace in public documents or everyday parlance during a particular period. In the end, my goal is to illuminate through poignant stories how life along the color line in rural Ohio has resulted in a population of persons who are both invisible and hyper-visual at one and the same time. My family has been firmly located in that Community Within.

INTRODUCTION

Almost instantly, I noticed the op-ed piece filling two-thirds of the page in this morning's *Columbus Dispatch*, both because of the headline that referred to "white innocence" and the photo of the guest columnist. The author, Renee, my colleague and an accomplished historian, wrote of the complexities of white folks' attitudes about race. While I always learn a lot from her precise scholarship, there was something about this particular missive that struck a chord. She wrote about her sense of a changing racial consciousness and awareness in white America that has even filtered down to rural Ohio where we are neighbors. It was this reference to attitudes about race in America's heartland that most interested me. Through a short vignette at the beginning of her article, she conveyed how she, a white woman from the Cleveland area, enjoyed taking the "back roads" when driving through our rural county, while her husband, an African American who was raised in the city, found such excursions to be stressful and potentially dangerous.

While I suspect that the primary thesis of Renee's piece was about how white privilege allows her to be more carefree while navigating her environment than is the case for her Black husband, I was struck by how much the narrative spoke to differences between African Americans who live or grew up in urban environments versus those of us who were born and reside in rural areas. It may not have dawned on

1

her that someone like me, Black and raised in a predominantly white, small town, might find driving through urban neighborhoods every bit as stressful and potentially dangerous as my big-city brethren might find just the thought of having their cars break down on one of those back-country roads. Is the terror and trauma of an unreliable vehicle more palpable when the highway turns to one lane and streetlights become nonexistent?

For years, I have read about racially based attacks upon Black men in urban areas like New York City's Howard Beach and Bensonhurst communities. These are neighborhoods entrenched in a northern, presumptively progressive city where violence against residents, including that which is racially motivated, was not an uncommon occurrence. The evidence is clear that violence against racial minorities has never been largely represented in, and definitely not exclusive to, less-populated regions of this country. So, it makes me wonder why people of color are more fearful of being victimized due to their race in rural environments where, even though there are substantially fewer people who look like them, there are also few, if any, incidents of race-based violence taking place in the vast majority of them.

Despite the prevalence of pop culture references to rural dangerousness, the facts don't bear that out. To the contrary, people who reside in rural communities, regardless of their race, ethnicity, religion, or other markers of difference, are substantially less likely to be victims of serious personal violence than are their urban counterparts. Yet, regardless of their place of residence, Black folks share a common burden of the weight of racism and inequality as well as the persistent threat of being victimized. While I may be as likely, perhaps even more so, than those in cities to have a racial insult hurled toward me in my small town, I'm not unduly concerned about being physically assaulted here for any reason, including because I'm Black.

Both the statistical reality and the perception that "chances are slim" that we will become victims of racial violence in our own communities may be a factor in dealing with racial animus for many of us who live in rural America. I suspect that for Black folks living in rural areas, one of the most distressing aspects of encountering racism in small towns is the pervasive sense of isolation. Not only do you carry the same burden as urban folks, you most often carry it alone. With a telling look while in the company of other Black people, a simple nod speaks volumes. Silently, we acknowledge each other's presence . . . each other's humanity; a meeting of the eyes is enough to say, "We're in this together." And, yet, we also are capable of understanding on those occasions when these gestures are not reciprocated that it doesn't necessarily mean that a person doesn't see their own Blackness or that they think that they are better than other Black folks. We can appreciate how difficult it often can be to let down the guard and embrace one's Blackness in a space where one has learned to be ever vigilant.

The changing faces of our community have complicated being Black in rural America. With a growing population of mixed-race people who in previous generations were subjected to the "one drop rule" and would have been labeled as African American, the complexion of Black America, both culturally and literally, has changed. Nowhere has that been more evident than in rural areas. Whether as a consequence of the significant absence of "same-race" prospects for partners or a lengthy history of mixed families in these communities, there has always tended to be a proportionately higher rate of mixed-race residents in small towns than in cities and the nation at large. Living within communities that are still operating within the limited and limiting binary of Black and white, many multi-racial persons are often not discernible by their white neighbors as African American or are otherwise regarded as racially ambiguous. Ambiguity, in this case, is truly in the eye of the inexperienced beholder. The absence of a mix of races and different ethnicities leaves small-town white folks struggling to look beyond the antiquated binary to acknowledge a multitude of difference. It isn't uncommon to hear them ask in the typical, insensitive fashion, "Where are you from? I mean, what are you?"

Long before I began to research and study the role and impact of race upon the lives of people of color, I felt it. I felt racial difference the way some feel the prickly itchiness of a woolen garment against sensitive skin. Never becoming comfortable but not quite sure if there is something less irritating with which to replace it. Having grown up in rural America, I felt it as a child in a space and locale that the majority of its residents assumed to be raceless. For me, however, it was every bit as much present as the rolling hills and fields that defined the geographic landscape that they occupied. I felt it as an adolescent, squeezing me like an unfamiliar piece of fruit seemingly out of place at the produce stand. But, it was me who was being told that I was out of place. I felt it as an adult in every waking moment like a burr that attached itself to my leg and couldn't be brushed off regardless of how hard I tried. Like a swollen tick that had grabbed onto my ankle just below the ridge of my sock, hidden just long enough to pose a risk of disease unless something was done swiftly and surely. With near surgical precision, we carefully pulled at its head to be certain to extract the entirety of the infectious carrion that threatened our lives. We took turns passing the tweezers from hand to hand defending one another from certain insult and injury. The only respite from this nagging self-consciousness about racial difference came within the close confines of my family, a mixed-race family where not everyone looked like me.

It is said that families form the backbone of American society. There is no question but that they are the lifeblood of Black communities across the land. Perhaps because of the lack of a critical mass of African Americans in many of the small towns that dot the landscape in this nation, the importance of families in establishing and maintaining Black communities in rural America cannot be over-stated. Mine was no exception. It faced a myriad of challenges that converged along the intersection of being rural, Black, and poor. For much of Black America, there is nothing particularly new or noteworthy about the latter two statuses or conditions. However, narratives about growing up Black in a small town in the Midwest are often far less known and even more infrequently shared outside our community. So, these tales of my family, comprised of plain ordinary people, are in many ways as much the stories of generations of families of small-town "cullud folks" as they are my own. And, perhaps surprisingly to some, they tend to resonate with plenty of rural white folks at times as well, a testament to the fact that in the end we have much more in common culturally than the things that are offered as proof that we are different. In the end, though, the color line remains.

CHAPTER 1

THE MAKING OF
LON HAMMONDS

As was common in many rural communities, adult children often built houses on land that was partitioned off from their parents' farmstead. In my family's case, my grandparents "gave" to their three daughters (the property records of that time often state "for the sum of $1 and love and affection") small contiguous parcels of land adjacent to their home in the Delmont Addition of Clinton Township, just outside the Mt. Vernon, Ohio, city limits. To some, this was a bit surprising since my mother and her two sisters were my grandfather's stepchildren, and he was already a father of three other children between his two previous marriages. Nonetheless, as my mother often reminded me, he was the most generous man she had ever known and felt lucky that he had come into her life so soon after her own father died. So, I grew up on a street that housed family members in modest structures on either side of ours. Two doors over was the main house that, despite a calamitous fire that burned it to the ground in the early 1920s, had pretty much occupied that space since the first decade of the 1900s. In an odd sort of way, I grew up in a "colored" section of my small town by virtue of the fact that there were Black folks spread across five households in our block, all of who were related by blood and marriage.

My grandfather, Leon Guthrie Hammonds (pronounced *Lon* and affectionately known to my mother as Lonnie), had migrated to Knox

FIGURE 1.1. Lon lands a job as cook for Camp Sychar.

County from Chillicothe, Ohio, where he was born in July of 1878. A handful of Black families had traveled up to Mt. Vernon from south-central Ohio in search of jobs in the town's two or three manufacturing concerns and founded the Mt. Calvary Baptist Church, only the second Black church in the county. Lon would have to wait his turn to land one of those prized factory positions, so he managed to bide his time doing what his mother, Rhoda, had taught him to do at a young age—cook. Early on, she noticed his keen interest in food; she figured he might as well learn to do more than just eat a lot of it. During a stint as one of the main cooks for Camp Sychar around 1900, he gained a bit of a reputation for his culinary skills. As a result of his contacts through the church camp, he began to pick up a smattering of catering jobs. He was known well enough that the local newspaper from time to time reported on his fine cooking or his involvement when he catered an event. With his jovial disposition and a booming voice to match, he was well liked in nearly every corner of the town.

Around 1916, Lon Hammonds managed to parlay his winning personality into a job at the Essex Glass Company. Unlike the few other colored workers at the glass plant, Lon managed to talk his way into

FIGURE 1.2. Lon Hammonds strolls down Main Street.

a skilled craft position as an apprentice "bottle blower," positions long dominated by the Belgian immigrants brought to the area for their experience and skills shaping glass. Whether it was luck or the efforts of his friend Samuel Payne, the first and only colored supervisor at the glass company, Lon steadily advanced in rank and seniority all the way into the early 1950s. Well into, if not beyond, normal retirement age, he seemed to defy his coworkers' expectations that he would one day tire of the hot, dirty work and step away from it all. The fact that he didn't was due, at least in part, to his daily routine of getting to work. It's quite likely that's what kept him going.

Neighbors would remark that they could hear Lon Hammonds coming from a mile away as he made the eighty-minute walk round-trip to and from his job by way of Pleasant Street. Ambling along a route with such an upbeat name was probably not a coincidence given Lon's positive disposition. You could easily hear him singing out loud or riotously laughing at his own jokes each step of the nearly two-mile commute from his home on the far-east side.

He was all business when he rose early each morning to start for work at 6 a.m., never once late for his seven o'clock shift. But the walk home usually involved several stops and occasional detours to exchange greetings with townsfolk and neighbors, especially the children for whom he never seemed to fail to produce a prized piece of candy or chewing gum after reaching deep into the pockets of his overalls. He surely had to be one of the most outgoing and popular men in the town. Like most successful colored folks, he had learned the lessons well that smiling broadly and engaging his neighbors in friendly conversation would often disarm white folks in his community enough to avoid confrontations or conflict.

Lon registered for the draft on September 12, 1918, even though he was already forty years old by that time. Even if it was unlikely that he would be called up for active duty at such an advanced age, Lon, like all colored men of his generation, knew that it was important to show his patriotism, even as the nation was in the throes of a pandemic and besieged by the Spanish flu. Ever mindful of how he was viewed by his white neighbors, it seemed that nearly everything he did reflected a sense of purpose to prove himself to be every bit as good as those around him. When the government asked, he and his family worked diligently to raise and maintain his "victory garden" to aid the US war effort during World War I. With food shortages common even in the States, he wanted to demonstrate that he was willing to make whatever sacrifice it would take to help the nation. His wasn't just a bountiful garden; it was a virtual showcase.

Within two months of Lon's registration and prior to his enlistment or orders to report for duty, Germany surrendered. Active military service wasn't to be for him like many others of his generation, too old to serve in this war and not born early enough to have been a Civil War veteran. So, he continued on at the factory, working the large press and blow machines that turned out glass bottles at what had become one of the major milk bottle manufacturers in the country. As a youth, I was delighted to find, on the few occasions when my grandmother allowed me to rummage around for glass remnants in her basement, some of his handiwork lined up on a shelf in the dirt cellar carved below their house. The old milk bottles, bearing the embossed

Essex logo or, later, the Lamb insignia, sit in my bookcases now and are among my treasured memories of her home at 8 Miami Street.

Lon Hammonds had achieved what Black folks had dreamed about and sought almost from the time they that they arrived up north in Ohio. The promise of landownership was more than just a road to economic independence and potential prosperity. In a way, it was a connection with the earth that had sustained them both across the sea and in a hostile, foreign world. Reaching down into the soil was the one constant that bound them to this place as well as the other. Despite the false promise of forty acres and a mule, people of African descent who crossed over the Ohio River and acquired small plots of land came to understand that, at worst, they could scratch out a modest living for their families and with luck, hard work, and God on their side perhaps much more. As my grandmother used to say, "There's soil, and there's dirt. One came from the other." I guess, for her, the closeness to dirt all those years as a maid wasn't as distasteful as I had once imagined.

Frugal almost to a fault, Lon saved and poured whatever money he earned into his homestead. He took tremendous pride in how he had built the various structures on his property. Even the chicken coops were elegantly crafted, getting fresh coats of paint and whitewash each spring. The gardens, orchards, and flowerbeds were meticulously attended. The more he was complimented on the beauty of his well-manicured estate, the more he worked to make it all the more spectacular. He built elaborate pergolas, trellises, lawn chairs, benches and swings, each carefully placed around his property. Statuaries and red brick planters topped with broad white bowls connected his prized peonies that ringed what to his grandchildren felt like a vast yard, especially for me after I became responsible for mowing it. Bulging river rocks encircled the beds of marigolds, pansies, and tulips. On the perimeter stood even more brick centurions with the smooth white domes serving as sentries against careless intruders. I was told that the look on his face as he surveyed his property showed that special pride he took in both his home and his country, having erected a towering flagpole that rose prominently in his side yard, guarded by a silver cannon that he had made himself in his sprawling yet tidy shop in the garage. For the

children, his elaborate bird house made to replicate the design of his home and that towered high above the outdoor privy was a feature of the property second to none.

Always a competitive person, Lon was obsessed with having the finest gardens and an immaculate yard. It wasn't enough that he knew that to be the case himself; he wanted the whole community to acknowledge his accomplishments. Despite the frequent compliments that his handiwork garnered, he wouldn't be satisfied until he was officially named the area's top horticultur-

FIGURE 1.3. Lon Hammonds' prized night-blooming cereus.

alist, at least in the colored community. To his dismay, that title seemed to go regularly to Charles Turner, whose prize-winning night blooming cereus was often featured in the local newspaper. Jealousy got the best of Lon, so he eventually raised two cereus plants that soon towered over his head.

He was sure that they rivaled anything that Turner, a founding member of the Mt. Vernon Colored Garden Club, had grown. Blooming only once a season on a single evening each summer, the whole neighborhood would descend upon 8 Miami Street to take a gander at the delicate white flowers that emerged. Long after Lon's death, my grandmother would grab her flashlight and head to the front corner of the house each evening in early July to look for blooms, something she had done with him for nearly two decades. As if by divine intervention, the miracle of those wondrous flowers was enough to rouse children in pajamas who were herded along by parents and grandparents from throughout the neighborhood to view the rare sight.

The combination of the park-like setting and Lon's reputation for putting on a spread made his home the place to go. Before long, he was hosting lawn fetes throughout the summer, featuring his expertly prepared refreshments against a backdrop of floral splendor. And it wasn't just the colored community that took notice. What made his soirees unique was that both Black folks and white folks from around the area attended those affairs. In fact, they often had more white folks on any given day, especially after he built a tennis court on the grounds.

At the request of his nephew, George Booker, Lon agreed to provide the land upon which a tennis court would be built if the young folks raised the funds to build and maintain it. In late spring of 1933, George had organized an entertainment program that featured a number of the local colored youth, including Lon's daughter, Agnes, who performed a rendition of "Underneath the Harlem Moon" with friends Ruth Ella and Helen Payne. Held at the meeting hall over the J. C. Penny store, it was a smashing success, attended by two hundred people and raising ample funds to undertake the project. His was one of only a couple of such courts in the entire town, so the area's leisure class, quickly becoming associated with the sport of tennis, frequented his home. My mother once recalled for me how as a girl she helped to load the bags of chalky lime into the cart that was used to carefully mark the lines that delineated the boundaries of play on the court.

Ever striving to climb the social ladder, Lon Hammonds was obsessed with replicating the various markers of respectability the white folks in the Knox County community had fashioned for themselves. Having and maintaining a fine home was only part of the battle. He financially supported the handful of Black secret societies like the Masons and Odd Fellows that began to sprout up in Mt. Vernon and other small towns. Even if he was reluctant sometimes to join these groups formally and be listed on the membership rolls, he agreed with their goals and wanted to register his approval. While cautious that he not be viewed as a social radical in a way that could harm his catering or lawn fete businesses, he heartedly subscribed to the notion that endeavors that involved music, literature, and other pursuits of

FIGURE 1.4. Marian Anderson concert program in 1930. Courtesy of Knox County History Society and Museum, Mt. Vernon, Ohio.

high culture would be the road to community-wide acceptance and prosperity for the local colored folks.

When the Booker T. Washington Club arranged for a concert by the venerable classical singer Marian Anderson in 1930 in Mt. Vernon, he and his wife, Ellen, were among the first to purchase tickets. Six years before the publication of the famed Negro travel guide, the Green Book, Lon and the other backers knew that Miss Anderson wouldn't be permitted to stay at a local hotel. So, plans were made to host her in the home of a local family. There was no home in the Black community more highly regarded than his. Although he was quick to offer his home to Miss Anderson, one of the ladies of the organizing committee insisted that their guest stay in her home. The widow Anna Sites' home was only a couple of short blocks from the Memorial Theater where the concert was to be held. Besides, it wouldn't be proper for such a dignified lady to stay over at this gentleman's home. While he lost the chance to show off his place at 8 Miami Street, he was somewhat relieved since none of his prized flowers would have been in bloom in March, and he would want his home to be seen in its full glory.

CHAPTER 2

DISCOVERING
THE REAL BERTHA

Once widowed and once divorced, Lon Hammonds had come to make a good living for himself and his family over the years. By the time that he met my grandmother, he was by all accounts a distinguished older gentleman. Regarded by the unmarried colored women around town as a good catch even as he neared sixty, he enjoyed the attention that he received from those who were forward enough to show their interest in him. But there was something about this newcomer in town who had recently visited his church. Unlike the handful of other unmarried ladies of the church, my grandmother seemed to pay him no mind. His frequent and obvious flirtations seemed to have little effect upon the mysterious woman who, he had learned, was boarding with Aunt Becky on the west end of town. Didn't she know who he was? How long could she possibly resist his charms? It likely was a combination of her light gray eyes that captivated him on the rare occasion when she was willing to look into his and the challenge posed by her seeming disinterest; he was immediately attracted to Bertha Fisher from the outset. In very short order, he had declared to his brother that she was "the one" and was dead set on getting her.

With jet-black, wavy hair that refused to stay tucked up under her hat, Bertha had a natural beauty that didn't require the assistance of fine clothes and piles of makeup, things that she couldn't have afforded even if she wanted them. She arrived in town from Coshocton, where she had gone to live with her sister, Leona, long before the untimely death of Arthur Fisher, her husband and the father of her girls. Art and Bertha had been going through some rough times in their marriage; she was tired of his infidelities and empty promises to put an end to them.

Making the decision to leave Barnesville to go live with Leona was hard enough; it was complicated further by the fact that Bertha was unable financially to take her two girls with her. So, her brother and his wife agreed to take one of them for a spell, and her father agreed to look after the other. She was to send for them when she found work and got settled. Leaving Art was also difficult because she still loved him. She, like many country girls, had the misfortune of falling for the first man to come into her life. He made her feel special, something that she had never experienced, and his attention was what she felt she needed more than anything else. Just as easily as he swept her off her feet, he repeatedly hurt and disappointed her. She hated to admit it to herself, but it soon became obvious to her and many others that he was perhaps the furthest thing from being a good husband. Every now and then, Art visited his estranged wife in Coshocton with promises to clean up his act and be true. Without question, she had had enough of him being unfaithful and knew deep inside that he'd continue to do wrong. But, damn it; he'd always been one smooth-talking rascal. She resented how easily he made her melt with his sweet words, piercing green eyes, and gentle kisses. As much as she wished it were otherwise, she came to expect that his way of making up always involved more talk than walk, and that what walking there was soon led to finding herself once again pregnant.

By the summer of 1927 during their on-again, off-again marriage, Art was, part of the time, back in Barnesville to work, when there was work. During the making-up part, he was back in Coshocton to sleep in his estranged wife's bed. It was during one of those latter times that Oneida, their youngest daughter, was conceived. Since her parents hadn't really reconciled, nor had her mother agreed to return and resume living with Art, their newest child was born in Coshocton,

where Bertha had decided to remain. As things turned sour in her sister's marriage, Bertha knew that continuing to live with Leona would
not be possible. The most pressing thing she faced by that time was to
find steady work and a place to live.

Finding a boarding house that would accept a child, one where
you'd even want to live with a baby, took some doing. Still holding out
hope that she would be able to send for her other girls, she struggled
to find enough work just to take care of herself and feed her newborn.
When Leona announced that she was moving to Cleveland, Bertha
knew that she couldn't hold down a job with a baby in tow. So, she
headed back home with her little girl to Center, an unincorporated
village that wasn't much more than a pass-through on the back roads,
in Belmont County between Warren and Barnesville. Hoping this was
just a minor, short-term setback, she was determined not to give up on
her plans to head back north to central Ohio, where jobs seemed more
plentiful than was the case in Barnesville. Reunited with her older girls
and living on the farm with her father by the fall, Bertha was disappointed that she was right back to doing what she had done before
she got away. In effect, she had simply picked right back up with the
same old stuff, returning to the world she had tried so hard to escape.
Being back on the farm scared her as much as it depressed her; she was
determined not to resume her former life. The only saving grace, if you
want to call it that, was that Barnesville was the site of an early Quaker
settlement where Black folks had settled after migrating up from the
South. The long-standing abolitionist sentiment alongside a relatively
early established Captina African Methodist Episcopal Church meant
that they weren't the only colored folks in the area and that not all of
the white folks were hostile to their being there.

By the following autumn, it became clear that no one would be
continuing or returning to their lives as they had come to know them.
In September of 1929, Oneida was barely 18 months old when the stock
market crashed. It didn't matter that nobody in her family had any
stock. None of them even knew exactly what it was nor had any idea
what it meant to own it, but the ramifications soon became clear across
the nation, even in her tiny corner of the world. The Great Depression

brought about massive unemployment and widespread poverty. Even for folks who had pretty much always been poor, this state of financial collapse brought new meaning to what it was to be destitute.

The utter despair and desperation on the faces of the jobless and homeless all around were frightening. Her family wasn't immune. Thank God for the farm and the crops they raised on their small plot of land, or they would have starved. Jobs in the area, for anyone but especially for colored folks, were for the most part non-existent. And it stayed that way for several years. Economic disaster tends to hit the working poor first and hardest; when the economy starts to recover, poor folks experience it last and feel it the least. Art had always had trouble holding down a steady job, and not much changed for him in the ensuing years. Other than not having to make the journey up to Coshocton to see his "girls," he could just show up at the farm, usually in time for supper, to check on his family. He was always ready and eager to spend the night, even if he wasn't invited.

Even though Art constantly reminded Bertha that they were still husband and wife, her plans were already underway to return to Coshocton. She didn't like feeling used; he disrespected her time and time again. Having town folks whispering about his drinking and running around on her motivated her to leave him every bit as the searing hurt that his unfaithfulness caused her. More than ever, she knew that the marriage wouldn't last much longer. She just didn't know that ultimately it wouldn't be a divorce that brought it to an end.

Bertha headed back to Coshocton and began saving up what money she could to hire a lawyer to file the divorce papers. A friend told her that there were a couple of families in Mt. Vernon, just up the road, who were looking for colored girls to clean and cook for them. She packed her trunk, arranged for a room at a boarding house, and managed to get a job right away as a maid. By the mid-1930s, as the economy began to recover a bit, she worked hard and, by word of mouth from satisfied employers, caught on in the homes of a few white families. Before long, she was sure that she would be able to send for her girls. She scouted around and managed to find a room for rent; she felt that she only needed enough space to get started. Sleeping four to

FIGURE 2.1. Bertha Hammonds in her work uniform.

a bed, she and the youngest at the head and the two other girls at the foot, it wasn't spacious but allowed them all to be together.

Bertha enrolled her children in the Fourth Ward School on the town's west side, not too far from Aunt Becky's boarding house where she had taken a room. Before the year was out, the two older girls decided they were done with schooling. Ina Mae, the oldest, had dropped out to take a job as a maid. Within months, she was married to thirty-five-year-old John Byrd, a member of one of the oldest Black families in the area and nearly twice her age. Mary Jane, the middle child who had just turned thirteen, found that her education included finding out how difficult life could become when pregnant at such a tender age. All of a sudden, Oneida no longer had her older sisters to walk her to the new school.

The call came from Bertha's sister-in-law, Murge. In between the sobs, she could barely make out the words, "There's been an accident." The story that appeared in the *Belmont Chronicle* on March 16, 1938, reported that there had been a truck accident while two colored men were out gathering scrap; in our family we had always called it "junkin'." The coroner's report listed the cause of Art Fisher's death as "crushed chest, internal injuries . . . run over by truck." Despite the statement in the paper that the death was accidental, rumor had it that Art was killed by the jealous husband of a woman to whom he was paying too much attention. It just so happened that the driver of the dilapidated pickup truck under which Art "accidentally" fell was his brother-in-law, Herman Edwards. And everyone knew that Herman's wife, Eva, was a fast and sassy number who liked to drink and enjoyed the attention of men, plenty of whom were quick to offer it. As a young woman, she was the kind of pretty that made others around her uneasy, not out of envy but out of sympathy, if you know what I mean. She learned early in life that her good looks could be used to both tempt and torment. Growing up in Coshocton, she married at 16, and folks said that she divorced soon thereafter under cloudy circumstances. It's always been pretty well known that shotgun weddings don't often last long.

Herman met Eva during a trip to Coshocton to visit his sister, Bertha. Before long, he decided to move there as well, taking up residence on Cemetery Street in the north end of town. He and Eva, who lived nearby, quickly became drinking companions. His drinking became routine and excessive; by the fall of 1931, Herman got a bit carried away with his favorite pastime and spent the night in Coshocton city jail for intoxication. This wasn't the first time that Herman had found himself involved with the law. According to the *Coshocton Tribune,* a quarrel over a woman left a colored man shot at the Herman Edwards home on Coe Alley just a few months earlier. The paper didn't give many details about the encounter, but it did specify that it involved a fight over permission to see a woman. By late 1932, Herman and Eva had moved in together, much to Bertha's chagrin. Now that he and Eva were keeping house, she'd have to see more of that woman than she cared to see. Her aversion to Herman's love interest might have been due to a rumor that Eva had become well acquainted with Art during one of his stays in Coshocton. Some said that was what led to her eventual breakup with her first husband, Clarence Mueller, with whom she had a daughter when she was sixteen. While some might have doubted that her reputation around town was capable of falling any lower than it already had by the time that Eva hooked up with Herman, her taking up with a colored man almost nine years her senior brought it down a few more notches.

In January of the next year under the headline "Negro Ordered from City," the *Coshocton Tribune* ran a short story in the News of the Courts section of the paper. "Herman Edwards, 27, colored, Cemetery St., was ordered to leave the city, and Mrs. Eva Mueller, 22, white, Elm St., was placed on probation after they pleaded guilty to charges of cohabitation in Mayor Johnson Smith's court Friday." It didn't much matter to the couple that Eva hadn't even gotten a divorce from her first husband; she had assured Herman that her marriage to Clarence had been over for some time. In her mind, there was no reason for them not to be together. But there was a reason; it apparently mattered quite a bit to the law, enough to bring the sheriff to their door. Adultery was a criminal offense. "Edwards was given his choice of paying a fine of $200 and costs or leaving the city and never returning. He chose to leave the city. Mrs. Mueller was placed on probation under a promise of good behavior in the future. The two were arrested at Edwards' home Wednesday."

White women in southeastern Ohio who kept company with Black men were often cast out by their families and shunned by so-called "self-respecting" white folks. It didn't matter to them that Art was the son of Sarah Ellen Tucker, an Irish-descended servant girl who happened to marry a colored servant in the household where they were both employed. It didn't make it any better that Bertha and Herman were also offspring of a white servant girl, Jennie Nancy Johnson, as well. The real surprise to most folks in town wasn't that Art had died young but that he hadn't been caught and strung up for his other dalliances in tiny Barnesville. Although Herman ultimately was the one to report Art's death to the sheriff, it was never quite clear just how that truck managed to crush his brother-in-law that frosty March morning. Bertha became a widow at thirty-eight, and her youngest daughter was only ten. My mother couldn't recall her father's death ever being discussed within the family from the day that the tragedy struck. When my curiosity got the best of me, I would ask her probing questions about her hard-drinking father who purportedly had a way with women. As if to protect the privacy and honor of her mother, or she just didn't want to believe that her father was a not-to-be trusted womanizer, she'd simply look away from me and say softly, "Well, I wouldn't know."

CHAPTER 3

TO WIN HER HAND

Lon Hammonds' ex-wife, Ethel, was a widow at the time they came together, having lost her spouse as he had recently done. She came from what many considered to be the most prominent and well-off colored family in the town. Her folks, the Simmonses, represented the closest thing to a "talented tenth" that this rural community would ever see. Her parents and uncles owned several properties and ran their own businesses. Her older sister was trained as a nurse, and her brother attended Oberlin College around 1902, beginning medical school before a tragic accident claimed his life. They were pillars in the church and leaders in most, if not all, of the colored societies and organizations in the community. The Simmons families had migrated to Mt. Vernon around the mid-1800s from Zanesville and farther south in Belmont County's Captina settlement near Barnesville, not far from the Ohio and West Virginia line. They were among the founders of the local AME church in the early 1870s. Ethel's father, Samuel Simmons, was the first colored child to graduate from Mt. Vernon's high school. And, he was determined that all of his children would do the same . . . and more.

Maybe it was Ethel's relatively privileged background that doomed the marriage from the start. While she had the social standing and pedigree that Lon thought he wanted in a wife, he discovered that she didn't relish the long hours and hard work that it took to maintain his slowly expanding estate. The only work to which she had become accustomed was giving piano lessons and managing the rental of rooms to boarders in the family's large and impressive home on South Gay Street. He hadn't expected her to balk at leaving her family's comfortable home nestled in the middle of the downtown area. It came as an unwelcome surprise to him that she wasn't the least bit interested in the country life that he had worked so hard to build. His house, as later explained to me by their only child, Dian, was much too far away from her family and downtown neighborhood friends for her taste. To his dismay, she frequently slept over at the Simmons' family house, perfectly at home sitting on the expansive wrap-around porch gossiping with anyone even remotely interested in the comings and goings of the town folks. After the birth of Billie Dian (the couple's nod to the light-skinned colored icon Billie Holiday), it became clear that Ethel had no interest in taking up residence way out on the edge of town. It wasn't long before Lon gave her an ultimatum: move in with him and take up her wifely duties or give him a divorce. She promptly declined to move into Lon's house and stay there to live with him rather than spending most of her time . . . and nights in town at her parents' home. Later on, he referred to the short-lived marriage to Ethel as his "leap year" marriage. The marriage lasted about that long.

The formal courtship between Lon and "Bertie," as he took to calling her in his constantly teasing, but affectionate, way, was quick. Lon wasted no time in looking for a new wife after his divorce in 1936. As much as he was drawn to the social status of Ethel, he was drawn even more to the work ethic of this younger woman to whom hard work was no stranger. Regardless of any intentions that he had about taking his third wife, Lon knew that Bertha was still married to her often-absent husband. After his repeated requests for her to divorce the lout and marry him, it didn't take long after Art's death that she finally gave in. They were married on the eighteenth day of July 1938, four months after she was widowed. At age thirty-eight and with three daughters, she felt fortunate to be marrying again, especially to a man who seemed to adore her, and, more importantly, had the ability to provide for her and her children.

Bertha had traveled to Mt. Vernon alone in search of work, assured that there were plenty of cleaning jobs in white folks' houses she could get. A quick remarriage changed her fortunes dramatically. It had been her goal to have her girls join her to begin new lives in this new area. Shortly after saying their "I do's," Lon told her it was time to bring the girls to live with

FIGURE 3.1. Lon and Bertha's gracious elegance.

them. While my mother, Oneida, was promptly enrolled at Hiawatha Elementary School, just a short distance from their home, Bertha's oldest daughter, Ina Mae, had dropped out of school by the eighth grade and began working as a maid. The middle child, Mary Jane, by that time sixteen, had already given birth to a daughter, Betty Lou, and would marry a year later. Barely seventeen, she would give birth once more and wed the father of her second child, a son, Arthur "Butch" Thompson. The following year, Ina married John Byrd, leaving Oneida as the lone child living with Bertha and Lon, except for those times when one of her sisters got divorced and moved in for a while.

As much as he would have preferred otherwise, Lon knew that Bertha's continuing to work as a domestic in the homes of white folks was an important contribution to the household. As he aged, he probably knew that it ultimately would become the steadiest source of income that they would have. He worked hard to try to let whatever pride he may have taken in her employers' occasional praise offset the lingering bitter taste of her having to cater more often to ungrateful people who thought that they were better than her. Bertha's work as a maid was many times more humbling for him than it was for her. It was the only work outside the home that she had ever known; in fact, she didn't know any working colored women who did another type of work. So,

FIGURE 3.2. Lon's house was a refuge and everything that Bertha wanted.

for her, it wasn't so bad, especially since it had given her the means to provide for her children, even in the most desperate times. It was abundantly clear that his house was his refuge, his fortress against slight and offense. Being home allowed them to retreat from being treated like menials. Still, there were a few reminders around the house like the handful of recipe cards that spelled out the ingredients for Mrs. Cassell's favorite salad, Mrs. Rahming's black bean soup, and other favorite dishes frequently requested by the white ladies for whom she cooked and did day work.

Throughout her older daughters' often tumultuous marriages, Lon and Bertha grew closer, bolstered by his supportive attitude and willingness to take the girls in. He was rewarded, as he had hoped, by her tireless energy to maintain their home. Having been raised on a farm, Bertha knew plenty about farm chores and wasn't the least bit hesitant to pull up her sleeves and get after them. On one day, she could tend to a bed of delicate flowers; on the next, she would get behind his three-tined plow and till up twenty rows for their vegetable garden. Every day, she would get out his aging wheelbarrow and fill up pails with water from the tin rain barrel at the corner of the house, hauling them across the yard to the south side of the chicken coop where the garden had been planted. Then she'd walk across town to clean someone's house and do their wash. And by the end of the day, she was hard at work to get supper on the table by the time Lon got home from work. Her skill in the kitchen was a consequence of having gained lots of practice as a teenager caring for her three younger siblings after her mother left the farm and then later for the various white ladies who employed her. Lon soon learned that Bertha wasn't hesitant to add her own touch to his home's décor. She had him build her a window seat with storage below it that stretched the entire length of the dining room. Taking full advantage of the sun that poured into the nearly floor to ceiling windows on the south side of the house, she grew and maintained an assortment of plants that made that room the most welcoming place in the house. The storage cabinets later became our secret hiding places despite her best efforts to keep us away from her carefully tended flowerpots. My mother would often tell us how much she regretted that she didn't inherit her mother's green thumb. Looking back, I realize now that I spent so much time at the dinner table when I was very young examining my grandmother's hands and then my own. Maybe, like many things, it skipped a generation.

The absence of Bertha's mother made her grow up quickly and learn to be self-sufficient. Still, it was the mystery of her mother's absence that was a much greater challenge than all of the household skills and chores she had mastered by the time she became an adolescent. Although her father, Elisha June, told others that he was a widower, it was more likely that Jennie left him and her kids. To this day, there is no record of when, where, or how this white farm girl from West Virginia died. She seemed to just disappear.

Over her entire life, and certainly well into her eighties, Bertha's smooth skin and sparkling eyes caused folks who met her for the first time to believe that she was many years younger than was the case. Fortunately, it ran in the blood as all three of her daughters maintained their youthful appearance for most of their lives, perhaps none more so than her youngest, Oneida. Bertha's face refused to betray what by all accounts had been a difficult life. From being abandoned by her mother to the shocking death of her young husband, she had already experienced enough crushing loss to last a lifetime. So, she often found herself turning to her father, June Edwards, for comfort and strength, all the while trying to remain upbeat and encouraging for her younger sisters and brother.

Bertha saw her father's own perseverance against the odds as her example. He taught her that she must always be cautious, especially around white people, even though many members of her colored family lived as white. Even neighbors could turn on you, he said, recalling the time that they came in the night. Torches in one hand and clubs in the other, the white men standing in the yard demanded that June come out and get what was coming to him. He laid low in a sunken hole under the porch, knowing that he was powerless to help Jenny if they decided to harm her as well. How she managed to convince them that June wasn't home that night and that she was willing to fight them all if they tried to come into their house, he never knew.

It must have been terrifying for June and his wife to know that if those men had set the house on fire that dreadful night that he would have been quickly swallowed up in the flames. He was sure, though, that all of it must have taken its toll on Jennie. She thought she was prepared for the taunts and the name-calling. She swore that the slights and the social isolation wouldn't bother her one bit as long as they could be together. Eventually, disowned by her family and shunned by what few friends she had, she began to show signs that the stress and fear of actual violence as a result of her interracial marriage had broken her down. Bertha took her father's life story as a lesson that no matter how much white people smiled to your face, it didn't take much to see behind the masks if you looked carefully. It's a wonder whether that lesson hit her even harder when she thought of the cruelness of her white mother having left her own children for reasons they never knew.

There could not have been a better role model for becoming a good homemaker than Bertha was for her youngest daughter. A self-described "farm girl," a label proudly passed down to her from her mother, Oneida took to the relatively privileged life on the Hammondses' estate. At least, it was privileged in comparison to what she had seen in her earliest years on Grandpa's farm back in Barnesville. She was born less than 18 months before the beginning of the Great Depression.

Already dirt poor, her family worked as subsistence farmers, producing just enough to get by. Down in Belmont County on Grandpa Edwards' farm, she was too young to have to shoulder any responsibilities as the older girls had done. Much of her time was spent "under foot" as her mother used to call it. She played and amused herself in the yard while her mother hung the wash on the clothesline, occasionally doing what toddlers do best, wandering off.

FIGURE 3.3. Oneida as a toddler explores Grandpa Edwards' farm.

One day, her frolicking took her over to the train tracks that separated her grandfather's farm from the adjoining property. She liked to pick up chunks of glistening black coal that had fallen off the railroad cars that sped by so fast. Perhaps, this was an early start on the primary family chore that she had later in her life, gathering coal to feed the pot-bellied stove that sat in the middle of the tiny house's main room. On this day, however, she failed to see the approaching locomotive. Even worse, her mother had lost track of the little one, unaware that her tiny daughter's life was suddenly in danger. With the train bearing down on her, a stranger came along and snatched her up and carried her off the track, just in the nick of time. Faster than Bertha could react and before she could show her gratitude, the man was gone. My mother told me that her family was convinced that it was one of the many jobless men who camped down by the tracks, sneaking onto passing trains to hitch a ride from town to town. Yet, no one saw him until the second that he saved the child, and no one saw him after.

I guess the near disaster left a permanent mark on Bertha's family. From that day forward, she would tell me, they never turned away a single drifter who needed a helping hand. Even though they were struggling themselves during the Depression, they had fruit trees on the farm and always raised a large garden each year. Sometimes she spent entire days picking and preparing the fruits and vegetables to be blanched and canned—what she always called "putting up." Fortunately, she repeatedly told me, our family never went hungry. Starvation didn't seem possible the way that my grandmother could manage to make a meal out of almost nothing.

Bertha became an expert in what she called "just gettin' by suppers." These were not fancy gourmet meals by any stretch of the imagination; they were the most basic of "fixin's." While she was soaking dandelion greens gathered in the backyard and telling her younger siblings hastily made-up stories about the night's meal, she managed to convince them that kings and queens probably wished they were lucky enough to have what the Edwards were having for dinner that night. To this day, I remember well the mush and milk that more often than I wanted appeared at our table. I'm sure that that was one way that she ensured that no one went to bed on an empty stomach. By the time that we came to live with her, she was a veritable magician with a bag of soup beans, fixing them every which way to Sunday. I'm sure that as a young woman trying to raise her younger siblings and, then, her own three children, those talents came in handy. I've held onto a few of my grandmother's recipes, carefully handwritten on the three-by-five file cards that my mother kept crammed in her wooden recipe box, an aging vessel made from inexpensive plywood and inexplicably inscribed with a misspelling of her first name. While I imagine that I might eventually attempt her signature spoon bread, I can't quite see myself putting to use the recipe for the scalloped brains casserole that led with the one-line admonition: "Clean Brains Good."

It was pretty common for one or more of the jobless men, who Grandma told me were called "hobos" in those days, to show up at their back door on the farm, standing with hat in hand while offering to perform work for a piece of bread. A piece of bread, mind you, not a sandwich. She'd mimic their words, drawing out each syllable so it sounded like the way that folks from down home talked. "Ma'am, I'm pretty good wit' a hammer and could fix that fallin' down fence if ya could just spare me's a plate-a beans an' maybe a biscuit." Even though they would sometimes spot one of the hungry men tugging at the fence to make it appear in need of repair, they didn't let on that they had seen it happen. Invariably, one of the children would be sent to the root cellar to fetch a jar of canned tomatoes, sweet corn, or pears. The men's eyes couldn't hide their surprise and excitement when they were told that they could have the entire contents so long as they brought back the jar. And they never failed to bring it back, even washing it out "real good" beforehand, she'd say. One older man, a regular in the transient encampment, carried his own broom with him everywhere he went. After receiving any amount of food, he would promptly sweep the porch of the house where he got it . . . that is, if it had a porch. Porch or no porch, he would always call out, "Thanks a million, ma'am, 'til you're better paid." That expression stayed with Bertha throughout her life and eventually was passed on to the rest of us.

Farm life to Bertha's family meant more than just not going hungry, although there was a lot to be said for that. The plants and the trees also provided comfort to the body in ways that few of them understood but upon which they all regularly depended. Grandpa Edwards was skilled in the ways of making potions by collecting an array of plants and herbs around the farm. He knew just where to dig to find the roots and bark to make a tea that would soothe an upset stomach. He knew that chewing on the leaves of a willow tree would provide pain relief for an aching farmer's back. My mother had been told that he learned the old ways from his Indian ancestors, people from whom her name, Oneida, was derived. Later, when a distant cousin informed me of his genealogical research locating our family's place within the indigenous diaspora, I learned that our native heritage likely traced to the Melungeon tribe. He told me that the Melungeons were a mixed-race people who descended in part from the Saponi and Catawba tribes of Virginia and the Ohio Valley. Regardless of where or from whom June Edwards learned the secrets of his medicinal alchemy, it was my Aunt Mary, my mother's sister, who told me how it was one of his concoctions that saved my mother's life during an especially harsh winter.

FIGURE 3.4. Grandpa Edwards with his two oldest children, daughters Bertha and Leona.

She was not quite two years old when Oneida came down with an illness that refused to be treated. Her skin felt as hot as a poker. And as her fever raged on, the old folks began to fear that the end was probably near for the sweet child. According to my mother's sister, Grandpa Edwards appeared in the doorway with a handful of herbs and twigs that he kept hanging in the cellar. He promptly boiled them in a small pot on the stove. Carefully, he dipped his long, checkered handkerchief into the mixture, dunking it slowly over and over again until every inch had soaked the liquid up. Then he stepped outside, kerchief in hand, testing it against his own cheek, until it was cool enough to tie around the little girl's neck. He lifted her limp body and placed the hanky loosely around her throat so that the tip rested on her upper lip just below her tiny nostrils. Then, in what seemed to be only a matter of minutes, the child's whimpering subsided and shortly thereafter the fever broke. The next morning, to the amazement of everyone and as if nothing had happened at all, Oneida got up from the bed and headed to what had been her usual place in front of the stove. "I'm cold," she said softly as she watched the flames lick the side of the steel potbelly.

CHAPTER 4

HELPING OUT
DURING HARD TIMES

Dealing with scarcity and limited resources wasn't anything new to Black families throughout Ohio, regardless of the general economic health of the nation. Those that lived in the small towns and hamlets developed strategies that combined both resourcefulness and the kindness of neighbors. Somehow, entire communities made up of persons often struggling as well took it upon themselves to make sure that whole families didn't go under. Whether or not such help went under the name "mutual aid societies" as they had done in previous generations, the effect was much the same. The type of competitiveness and selfishness often associated with urban life where large numbers of people tended to work and live among relative strangers was for the most part absent in the rural areas. Thus, as colored folks picked up and moved from one small town to the next, they were often welcomed and kindly received by the handful of other residents, particularly by members of the local churches. Most Black communities in Ohio's small towns had at least one church; some had two, usually a Baptist Church and an African Methodist Episcopal Church. These were the usual jumping off points for new arrivals. While ministering to the soul, it was equally important for the church to lend a helping hand when folks got down on their luck, whether it be pitching in to help harvest crops during times of illness, scraping together some funds to meet

FIGURE 4.1. Lon was committed to the Mt. Calvary Baptist Church.

an overdue mortgage payment, or coming up with burial expenses for those who died alone without any kinfolk nearby.

Barely sixty miles northwest of Grandpa Edwards' farm in Belmont County and a short ride east of Mt. Vernon was the little town of Coshocton where the Sheffield-Graham family came to settle. In search of a steady, decent-paying job, Sam Sheffield migrated north from Virginia and West Virginia to join his sister in Youngstown, Ohio. There can be no question that the residual effects of slavery and the subsequent indentured labor that Black folks suffered lasted for generations after official manumission. The deleterious impact upon the health and well-being of nominally free men and their offspring who continued to work in the fields and mines of former slaveholders and their descendants was readily apparent. These men often died younger

than they should have while their families mourned more often than
ought to have been the case. It wasn't until much later that Sam would
come to know what damage the coal dust had done to his lungs. Perhaps that played a large part in his decision to join the great exodus
of Black folks out of the South and eventually landed him in north-
central Ohio where he had relatives who had headed north a few years
earlier. It was a beautiful region of the state accentuated by heavily for-
ested hills and fertile farmland. And unlike much of the declining areas
of Kentucky, Virginia, and West Virginia from which many of them
came, it seemed that every able-bodied person had a chance at landing
a job and making a good, or at least better, life.

Tillie Mae's journey into Ohio was prompted by a revival camp
meeting in Youngstown at which she was to perform. Despite being
recently widowed after the death of her husband, John Graham, she
felt compelled to continue the Smiley family work of saving souls. The
mission was righteous. Yet she also knew that she derived comfort in
her faith and her faith was its strongest when she was singing. She was
convinced that God would show her the way to survive the loss of her
husband. With no choice but to put her trust in the Lord as she tried
to find a way to care for her five children, she could not have predicted
that He would have an answer so quickly. Sam's sister, Stella, attended
Tillie's singing performance at that Youngstown camp revival. Encouraged by his sister to accompany her to the following night's meeting, Sam reluctantly agreed and certainly was not at all disappointed.
Afterwards, he told his sister that not only could this evangelist sing,
but she "was the prettiest thing" that he had ever seen. He insisted
that they hang around to meet her, which they did. Whether it was
the siren call of her piercing voice or the irresistible compulsion of the
Holy Ghost, Sam was smitten. They were married three weeks later
and eventually brought all five of her children to Coshocton to join
them.

The opportunity to get by and support one's family remained true
for the first few years after the Sheffield-Graham family arrived in
Coshocton. Things, however, changed drastically by the end of the
decade. It is a marvel that Sam and Tillie managed to support a house-

hold of eleven when the Great Depression hit. Of course, in the face of the enormous pressure that the couple felt, they knew that they couldn't do it alone. In addition to the six children living under their roof, there were other adults in the household who were working as well to help the family survive. Even though one of them, Tillie's dad, Pop Smiley, was too old and Sam's brother, Hobart, too ill to help much, everyone tried to chip in. Most of couple's sons worked as janitors or did odd jobs; Tillie and her daughters who were old enough did day work as domestics. As uncertain as things were at times . . . well, most of the time, they managed to keep a roof over their heads and put food on the table. Things went along like that for quite some time. Even a decade later, things were still difficult financially for the Sheffield household.

By the late 1930s, things were slow to improve much financially at his parents' home. There would be no carefree days during his teen years, so Sam Jr. dropped out of school after the eleventh grade to enter the federal government's Civilian Conservation Corp. The CCC was a New Deal WPA assistance program intended to put able-bodied men to work on government projects. When asked about his age, he had no qualms about lying to appear older than he was. He was promptly assigned to a company to work with other colored corps members in Zanesville planting trees on what had to be one of the largest tree farms in the nation. While the work was, for the most part, mindless even if oftentimes backbreaking, he took some solace in knowing that twenty-five of his thirty-dollar monthly pay was being automatically sent back to his mother. He took comfort in knowing that he could do his part, and there would be one less plate at the table for a meal or two each day. Hoping to make some additional money, he hired on for any odd jobs that came his way. When those jobs dried up, he began to feel desperate. So, he swallowed his pride and got a job as a shoeshine boy at the downtown shine parlor. That was harder than he had first imagined, not physically but psychologically. It was one of the most humbling moments in the young man's life. Maybe, he had been just fooling himself to think that he would eventually see that bright future that was forecast for him come to fruition one day. Even the intermittent jobs he got as an unskilled laborer washing and greasing cars in garages did not feel as demeaning and demoralizing as this one.

As the eldest son of a Baptist minister, Sam grew up in a strict, religious household. His adventurous spirit made conforming to his parents' rules of the house difficult during his late teens. He rebelled in small ways when the opportunity presented itself, which for him wasn't often enough, and he became increasingly jealous of the relative freedom that the other boys in his neighborhood seemed to have. From his friends' stories about throwing rocks at garages or knocking over gravestones in Oak Grove Cemetery, he longed to experience some excitement in his life and shed the restrictions attached to being the preacher's kid. After dropping out of school and joining the CCC, he found himself surrounded at work by men much older than he was. He regularly hitched a ride to and from the camp in Zanesville with some of those guys from Coshocton. After the day's long toil, the guys were often in the mood for some fun. Their idea of entertainment after work was much more adult than what he was accustomed to and nearly always involved drinking.

Drinking booze wasn't commonplace at his house. Despite his parents' public piety, he knew that on special occasion they would imbibe a little every now and then, especially his dad. After all, his dad grew up in the hills of Virginia and, later, labored as a young man in the coal mines of West Virginia where the moonshine they called white lightnin' held sway. With Sam Sr. still a few years away from taking up his calling to the pulpit, he had plenty of chances to become acquainted with the allure that alcohol had in his customary surroundings. As the good reverend discovered, his pious wife, Tillie Mae, proved to be much harder to coax into letting her hair down when it came to having a drink. The reverend had to admit that on more than one occasion he secretly hoped that she might come down with a cold so that he could convince her that sipping on a hot toddy would help to put her on the road to recovery. During their time working at the Coshocton Country Club, Sam was expected to tend bar for club events in addition to his janitorial and handyman chores. He, admittedly, enjoyed this assignment a bit more than his wife thought that he should. As a member of the local chapter of the Woman's Christian Temperance Union, she believed that drinking could lead to the destruction of civil society and was a particular threat to colored families. As a devout Christian woman, it was her duty to convince him that it didn't look good for a minister to be serving alcohol. And, she did.

FIGURE 4.2. Rev. Sam and Tillie Mae in the parlor at the Coshocton Country Club.

CHAPTER 5

MORE THAN JUST FAITH
ON TRIAL

It didn't take long for Sam Jr. to come to realize that drinking and carousing with a bunch of guys in need of some fun could lead to serious trouble. On an unusually hot Thursday night in mid-June of 1940, Sam and the fellows from his neighborhood were sitting on the front porch at Charlie Williams' house on North 6th Street as they so often did in the summers. They would take turns sitting on porches at each other's houses until the old folks came out and shooed them away for roughhousing or being too loud. Usually, they would head off to the vacant lot to play some ball if it wasn't too hot. On really hot nights like this one, the only exercise that appealed to them or they could muster was fanning themselves with the old, ripped-up magazines traded from household to household and left piled up in the corner of the porches for easy borrowing.

Chappy, the name by which he was best known, and his Williams family recently moved north to Coshocton from Alabama. They lived in a house directly across the street from the entrance to Oak Grove Cemetery. One of the boys sprawled out on the porch swing said he saw Eddie Johnson heading into the cemetery at the end of their street. As a way to discourage rowdiness and vandalism, a local ordinance made it illegal to go into the cemetery after dark. Eddie, one of the few white guys living on their end of the street, stayed with his 72-year-old

FIGURE 5.1. Sam Jr. and his denizens of the diamond.

grandmother at 236 N. 6th Street, just a block south of Sam's house. Nobody knew just why he lived there, but rumor had it that his mom had him while she was 17, not long after a shotgun wedding to his father. The couple moved in with her mother; thirty years later, nobody knew what became of them. So, Eddie shared this rundown house with the old lady alone, even though he didn't care for her rules about no alcohol and no entertaining girls. He was in the company of a woman when he appeared at the cemetery, and the boys were sure that could mean only one thing.

Things went wrong that night, very wrong for Sam and his friends. There is no way to know for sure what exactly happened. Did they follow Eddie and his female companion into the graveyard to spy on them, hoping to catch sight of some heavy petting, if not a glimpse of her naked body or perhaps even watch them engage in sex as young boys were wont to fantasize about? Did they ask for a swig of some of the alcohol that the two had with them and which they had clearly consumed in large quantities before they arrived? Did they spend time hanging around and drinking with the two adults? Did they catch them in the act of intercourse and boldly propose that one or more of them join in the fun? Whatever transpired that night, one thing is for sure. They were about to fall into a nightmare that even the most active imaginations of boys on a lark in a cemetery at night could possibly conjure up.

Within hours, forty-five-year-old Vivian Schaeffer claimed that she had been raped late that evening by several colored boys in the Oak Grove Cemetery. Despite her making some startling and very serious allegations, her story didn't seem to make much sense even to the law enforcement officers who investigated. During the questioning, each statement she made was inconsistent with her previous one. She couldn't satisfactorily explain just what she had been doing in the closed cemetery so late at night, what had happened exactly, who had done what, or why she was with an intoxicated man drinking alcohol with him there after hours. Her memories weren't very clear about that evening, and they weren't helped by the amount of alcohol that she had consumed.

Notwithstanding their concerns about the truthfulness of the allegations, the police began to round up a number of colored boys who fit the description, descriptions helped along by Eddie Johnson who lived in the neighborhood and knew most of the boys on sight as well as by name. For the entire Black community, the shock of these charges was heightened by the chilling similarities to a high-profile racial injustice that had occurred just a few years earlier. Reminiscent of the infamous Scottsboro boys case out of Alabama in which a group of nine Black boys were accused of raping two white women on a train, local folks here knew how that turned out and were also keenly aware of the Klan's history in their own county.

The Coshocton case brought against these seven young Black males wasn't just shocking, it was eerily similar to that case out of Alabama, the state where both Chappy Williams and his friend and fellow-accused Rush Hargrove's father were born. The alleged victim in the case against the Coshocton boys, like the Alabama case, was also a white woman accompanied by a white man; yet, this local man's role at the time of the alleged crime, whether as her failed protector or as a willing participant, was never revealed in the case at hand. Did Eddie, like any self-respecting white man, valiantly fight the colored boys to protect this white woman from being so brutally ravished? Did he commit the unthinkable and become an accomplice to the outrage? The eventual outcome of the case suggests that his credibility as a witness had been as much in doubt as was hers. Still, that wasn't enough to stop the case from proceeding nor was it enough to ensure that justice would ultimately prevail.

The newspaper reported on June 15th that four of the boys, including Sam, pleaded guilty, and the other three pleaded not guilty. For more than three months after charges were brought in the Mayor's Court, six of them languished in the Coshocton jail unable to raise the $1,000 bond. The seventh, Rush Hargrove, one of the three who pled not guilty, was fortunate. His family put up their house as surety in order for him to make bond on that Saturday when the boys were rounded up and arrested. By doing so, he was spared from having to await trial in jail. This apparently saved him from the same fate the others must have suffered that first night while in custody of the local sheriff eager to get to the bottom of the case. It likely also aided him in ultimately having the case against him dismissed. He was the only one of the boys who was not convicted of an offense arising out of those charges. Whatever took place during the arrest or during the first night in jail was not made part of the official record. No one witnessed the interrogation; no signed confession was ever produced. No one will ever really know what was said or done to the boys, but whatever it was led to having four of them confess to a heinous crime.

Despite alleged confessions on the evening of the arrests, it wasn't until the following September, a full twelve weeks later, that the Coshocton County grand jury returned indictments against six of the boys. Set to face trial were Lindy Meredith, Robert Taylor, Donald Taylor, Eugene Taylor, Charles Williams, and Sam Sheffield. There was no explanation for the delay in presenting the case to the grand jury;

yet, exactly one week from the day the indictments were handed down, the case was closed. The highly irregular handling and outcome gave a hint that there were problems with the state's case against the boys. The prosecuting attorney, Carl Patterson, stated that the case was filled with "confusing circumstances . . . and conflicting stories." By his own admission, these things "made it difficult to determine how many [and, therefore, which] of the Negroes accomplished the act of rape." Therefore, the prosecutor was willing to accept a plea of guilty to reduced charges in order to resolve the matter. For such serious charges, it must have been a tremendous surprise to many in the town that the case would end abruptly with Judge Daugherty accepting the deal. Few, though, concluded that it may have had something to do with the lack of evidence that any of the boys was guilty as charged. The absence of public condemnation of the injustice done to those boys should not have come as a surprise, but the lack of an outcry that nothing was done to more severely avenge the indignities allegedly perpetuated against the woman spoke volumes about what was generally believed to have been the truth. The lack of any punishment after conviction could have only meant that there was no evidence of a crime whatsoever.

What could have compelled a white prosecuting attorney in a predominantly white, rural town to reduce the charges against a group of Black boys accused of raping a white woman? If any of the charges were even the least bit true, then it is inconceivable that a case of this notoriety could have ended in such a manner. Perhaps the answer lies in things that were operating behind the scenes the way many legal matters frequently get handled. These boys didn't have any special standing in the community. There were few, if any, colored folks in all of Coshocton with the kind of connections or influence that could have affected the outcome of a case like this. Even if there had been, these guys weren't thought to be in any of those families with the possible exception of Sam Sheffield. Fiercely handsome and popular about town, Sam wasn't the kind of young man who got into serious trouble of any kind. It was hard to believe that someone as well-liked and from a devoutly Christian home as he was could do such a thing. It all seemed so out of character.

At the time, it was unclear as to who made the arrangements or how they came to be, but all of the sudden the accused found themselves represented by a young attorney, Lawrence Burns. It's not known whether Burns asked for or was paid a retainer for his representation. It isn't clear who could have paid it had one been required. Yet, Attorney Burns likely was no stranger to Tillie Sheffield given that they would have previously crossed paths at local Republican Party functions. That prior acquaintance was likely a key to her being a bit more comfortable with placing the fate of her son in the young lawyer's hands. Although only seven years into the practice of law, Burns was known as an extremely sharp and effective lawyer. Perhaps more importantly, he had begun to climb the professional and social ladder in Coshocton. Down the road, his legal talents and personable disposition served him well statewide when he eventually was elected president of the Ohio State Bar Association. It would become apparent much later how or why he just happened to show up one day to enter his appearance on the record as their counsel.

Lawyer Burns, an Ohio State law graduate, was politically astute and becoming increasingly well connected. Another OSU law graduate, William Pomerene, couldn't help but be impressed. When the call came from Mr. Pomerene, senior partner of Pomerene & Pomerene, about needing his help with a local criminal case, Burns began to realize that this might have been his chance to make a name for himself in the highest echelons of the Coshocton legal community. The Pomerene name represented one of the most successful and influential families in the town. Judge Julius Pomerene was the area's most respected jurist in the late nineteenth century. After leaving the bench, he opened up a new law practice that eventually saw his older son, William, join his firm. The Pomerene prominence grew when William helped found the Coshocton National Bank, serving as its vice president. Younger brother Frank, who had joined the law firm, was appointed to a seat on the board of directors of the bank.

Lawyer Burns wasn't sure why he was encouraged by Mr. Pomerene to represent a group of local colored boys accused of such a heinous act. While that might ordinarily have proven risky for a young attorney's reputation, if not an outright social liability, the fact that the request was coming from William Pomerene lessened his concern. If this pillar of Coshocton's upper-crust society was making the request, then he wasn't going to worry about how it would affect his own standing in the community, whether in the present or the future.

William Pomerene's intervention in this case was a major influence. Beyond their business and social prominence, members of the Pomerene family had always had political aspirations as well. One cousin, Atlie Pomerene, had served as Ohio's lieutenant governor in 1910 and was later elected to the United States Senate. Atlie, who lived in Millersburg in adjoining Holmes County, ran unsuccessfully in 1928 against then New York governor Al Smith for the Democratic nomination for president of the United States. Smith was later defeated by Herbert Hoover for the presidency. Pomerene's political career did not end there since Hoover, although a Republican, tapped him in 1932 to lead the Reconstruction Financial Corporation. In addition to being elected Coshocton County prosecuting attorney, a position he held until 1898, William Pomerene was elected president of the board of trustees of the Ohio State University, his alma mater. This was no ordinary family. So, when its patriarch called upon Burns, he felt that it was in his best interest to listen and assent to any request made of him.

Initially, Burns wondered if some of the local elites were concerned about the case's potential impact upon the town's reputation following the US Supreme Court's rebuke of the prosecution in the Scottsboro case in Alabama just a few years earlier. He, himself, had become active in the county's Republican Party and was well aware of how his party tried to promote itself as being more supportive of civil rights than the Democratic Party was. Since the late 1870s, as Black men gained the right to vote, they had been solidly loyal to the party of Lincoln. After women gained the right to vote in 1920, Black women became tireless workers for the Republican Party. By the late 1920s, one such worker in the tiny town of Coshocton was Sam's mother, Matilda Mae Sheffield.

Almost from the time she and her family arrived in Coshocton around 1920, the year that the 19th Amendment was passed ensuring women the right to vote, Tillie Sheffield became politically active. She immediately began serving on committees and attending events for the county Republican Party. Like the men of her community, both in Kentucky and Ohio, Black women were loyal supporters of the Republican Party since the late 1800s. Now that they had the right to vote, they would prove themselves important allies to the party of that great Republican president, Abe Lincoln. Tillie was a natural. Some might say that her organizing and leadership skills were an outgrowth of her many years of being on stage singing at religious revivals. They also came with the solid encouragement of her father, Reverend Charles Bell Smiley, to forever be in the service of lifting up her people as she sang the praises of her Lord.

Tillie Mae was the jewel of the extraordinary colored Smiley family from Louisville, Kentucky. As the youngest daughter of Charles and Eliza, she was a more-than-willing recipient of all the attention that her parents and older siblings could bestow upon her. The members of the local Republican Party in her new hometown of Coshocton could never have known how personal Tillie's commitment to their political party was. Looking back, perhaps, it was her way to show her eternal gratitude to the great emancipator. It was as if her service to the party was done in repayment for the legal manumission of her mother, her greatest inspiration who had passed away just a couple of years earlier.

The story that motivated Tillie to become active in the Republican Party had been passed down for years in her family in that bluegrass state just across the river from Ohio. According to family lore, her father, Charles Smiley, had courageously rescued an enslaved girl, Eliza Jane, from Dr. Lenis J. Frazee's household. More than half a decade after the constitutional prohibition of slavery, Frazee had the audacity to declare to the census taker that the fifteen-year-old mulatto girl inhabitant of his household was his "domestic servant," a cynical reframing of indentured servitude that at least officially replaced the shackles. After spiriting her away from her previous enslaver, the not-so-good doctor Frazee, Charles married her and vowed to protect her from harm for the entirety of her life. And the couple had the good fortune to bring into the world Tillie along with her seven brothers and two sisters. Despite his admitted earlier larceny involving his

future wife, "Pop" Smiley eventually heeded the call to join the pastor-
ate and founded the Hill Street Baptist Church in Louisville. But it
was Tillie's brothers, renown in the region after they formed the famed
quartet the Ballard Chefs, who exposed her to her life's calling when
she heard them perform. They managed to use their singing success to
land highly respected and coveted positions as Pullman porters on the
Louisville and Nashville Railroad. Her oldest brother, John, was one
of the creators of the seminal Baptist hymnal known as the Gospel
Pearls in 1921. Published by the National Baptist Convention USA, it
would be the first time that the term "gospel music" was mentioned in
print in America. Sitting in front of the old family radio during her
brothers' weekly Monday broadcast on station WHAS, she knew from
that point on that she would put her voice in service to the Lord and
her people.

A member of the Ohio Association of Colored Women, Tillie Sheffield took to heart the organization's creed, "Lifting As We
Climb." Others could tell just by being in the presence of this incred-
ibly strong and confident woman that she was made to be in the spot-
light. On a number of occasions, she organized the entertainment for
the local Republican Party's rallies. It was in his role as a party official that Attorney Lawrence Burns would have had an opportunity to
meet and interact with Tillie. In addition to her association with the
party, this woman also held leadership positions in local colored wom-
en's clubs and seemed to have formed relationships with highly placed
white women and influential women's organizations all over the city.
The list of celebrations, clubs, churches, and private events at which she
sang was long and impressive. It was as if she had as her personal goal
to sing at least once at every Christian church in the county, and she
nigh well succeeded. She was easily the most recognized gospel singer
in the area. And, sacred music was her calling card.

Whatever political motivations might have played a part, this highly
improbable assignment given to Burns may have been much simpler
than all of that. Perhaps, it was not the consequence of political favors
or strings being pulled out of unspecified obligations. It is quite possible that William Pomerene had a personal reason for intervening;

maybe, he was doing it as a favor and at the request of his maid, that same Tillie Mae Sheffield, for whom he was very fond. In fact, there were also other connections between his family and hers. His cousin Atlie had in his employ a colored man named Crawford Williams. Williams was married to Vivian Graham, Tillie's daughter and Sam Jr.'s half-sister. Crawford was Atlie's personal chauffeur. Another reason may have been the fact that Reverend Sam Sheffield was the personal chauffeur for the Broome and Herbig Company in the early and mid-1930s. Henry C. Herbig, the company's president, was an officer in the Coshocton National Bank in which William Pomerene was the founding vice president. It is quite likely that he, too, would have been sympathetic as well to the plight of his former driver's eldest son. While these colored men had no special social standing and had little financial means, their service and loyalty may have been rewarded by these men of influence, enabling them to get much better results than they could have bought or mustered on their own.

What exactly went down during that second week of September 1940 will never be known; the facts as they transpired between Prosecutor Patterson and Attorney Burns in all likelihood went to the grave with them. We'll never know if the experienced former prosecutor, William Pomerene, placed a call to Patterson . . . or the judge . . . to offer some advice. It will never be known if the boys protested or balked when asked, or were pressured, to plead guilty to crimes that they didn't commit, even if they would only be doing it to have the charges reduced. Who knows what outcomes they were promised or if, after three months in jail, they were guaranteed not to have to spend any more time behind bars? How often have frightened Black youth, threatened with possible life imprisonment or the mention of a death sentence, been willing to do or admit to anything if they thought or were told that it would make all of their troubles go away? Did they know that a Black man accused of raping a white woman had been lynched in their little town a few decades earlier? It didn't matter then, perhaps now, if he was innocent.

What is known is that Judge Daugherty accepted the plea agreement struck by the prosecuting attorney and the boys' defense counsel.

As a consequence, all six of them pled guilty and were convicted of assault with intent to commit rape. It would be nearly fifty years later in a case known as the "Central Park jogger case" that the general public in this nation would gain greater insight as to how innocent boys could confess to a crime that they did not commit. Despite the fact that the Coshocton boys were offered a chance to plead to these lesser offenses, these were still very serious charges to which they were confessing. It will never be known how heavily the gravity of these convictions weighed upon their hearts or affected them for the rest of their lives. The fact that innocent Black youths were never cleared of the false charges nor able to reclaim their good names meant that a stain would forever remain on the entire town, a town whose best-known landmark, Roscoe Village, ran the length of the road officially, if not more than a bit ironically, known as Whitewoman Street.

Judge Daugherty's announcement the day of sentencing rang hollow. "Whatever the character of the complaining witness in this case, she was entitled to protection of the law. She had no business in the cemetery at that time with an intoxicated man and a quantity of beer. It is very clear here that there was an assault but I believe that the prosecuting attorney is right in accepting a plea to this lesser charge . . . It has been my policy to give all boys coming before this court for the first time a chance. The fact that these are colored boys makes no difference—we do not hold that against them. It will be the sentence of the court that all of you will be placed on probation, with imposition of sentence deferred on condition that you remain law abiding citizens, return to work and avoid late hours. By that I mean that you should be home by 12 midnight. Each of you must pay the costs in this case and report to the sheriff three times a year for five years." As if to emphasize the seriousness of the crimes for which they were convicted, and in stark contrast to the lenient sentences, the judge warned the boys that he would send them to the penitentiary for up to ten years if they violated the terms of the probation. Ten years for failing to hold down a job or staying out late compared with mere probation for allegedly trying to rape a white woman? "Four of the six boys told the judge that they expected to return to jobs they held before their arrest. The other

two declared they intended to enlist in the army." True to their promise, Meredith, Williams, and the Taylor boys either returned to their
old jobs or managed to get others. Sam and Eugene immediately made
plans to enlist in the service.

Oh, and the alleged victim and her companion? Vivian Schaeffer
was charged with committing a crime of her own in connection with
the events of that shameful evening: "trespassing in a cemetery during the night season." She was fined twenty-five dollars and costs after
pleading guilty. Although the local newspaper was silent about when
and for what she had been arrested, "she was returned to city jail to
serve out the fine when she was unable to pay." This highly unusual
and suspect outcome in a case of this type made it quite clear that she
wasn't treated like the typical victim of sexual assault. Had there ever
been another case in the entire nation where an alleged victim of rape
was cited, fined, and jailed for a misdemeanor offense arising out of
the events of such a crime? And, what happened to her male friend?
"Eddie Johnson, Miss Shaffer's (sic) companion in the cemetery, was
fined $25 and costs and given 30 days in the workhouse on charges of
trespassing in the cemetery and intoxication. Johnson first must pay or
serve out the fine and costs in city jail here after which he will be taken
to Columbus to serve the workhouse sentence, the mayor said."

CHAPTER 6

SEWING ON THE STRIPES

In November of 1940, eighteen-year-old Sam Jr. registered for the draft. With few job prospects and this frightening brush with the law still fresh in his mind, he decided to follow the lead of his older half-brothers and enlist in the army. In fact, his registration card bore the name of his half-brother John Graham as the person with whom he lived and who should be contacted in order to reach Sam. Whether he had moved out of his own accord or was banished from his parents' home after being released from jail wasn't clear. What was clear was that his parents were relieved that he was getting out of Coshocton. They knew now from personal experience that unemployed Black men in that small town were bound to get into trouble whether they were at fault or not. It was just a matter of time. Sam's scrape with the law was more than just painful for them as parents; it also was a source of major embarrassment for his reverend father and evangelist mother. As my Uncle Maurice, who was only twelve at the time, later confided to me some eighty years later, "Mother said that 'it was over,' and that we were never to speak of it again. And, to my knowledge, none of us ever did."

In addition to being leaders of their church and prominent in religious circles throughout the area, Sam's parents had invested themselves heavily in climbing the social ladder in this town. It was important to

FIGURE 6.1. It was important to Reverend Sheffield
to be seen as a pillar of his community.

them, perhaps too important, that they be admired and respected in both the Black and white communities. Tillie regularly was referred to in the social pages as "the distinguished wife of Rev. Sam Sheffield." This episode with her son surely was not the type of publicity or distinction that she so often sought. Sadly, it may well have been that at the time they were even more concerned about their standing in the community than in the well-being of their son. How dare he be so reckless and selfish to risk so much for all of them, to undo the gains that they and other respectable colored families had made. Fortunately, even if inexplicably, the judge had agreed to sentence him to probation on the promise that he found work or went to the army. With more than a little nudge from his parents, it was clear what he had to do.

After arriving at Coshocton's local draft board, he was promptly scheduled for the entrance exam the following week. On December 5th, he reported to Fort Hays in Columbus for the exam. After seeing how well he scored on the written exam, the recruiter asked him why he didn't finish his schooling first. Sam said he intended to go back, but for now he needed to lighten the load on his family. Although he didn't say it aloud, he also was anxious to get far away from a town that wouldn't hesitate to bring charges for any, even no good, reason against colored men if given a chance.

By February, Sam, Jr. became an enlisted man and promptly assigned to the 364th Infantry, Company F. Even though nearly all of Europe was at or about to go to war, he didn't envision himself ever seeing battle. His first stop found him at Fort Huachuca in the mountains of the southeast corner of Arizona. A product of the Indian wars of the late 1800s, and for twenty years the home of the 10th Calvary Buffalo Soldiers, Fort Huachuca's environment could be as physically challenging as any installation in the nation. Due to the elevation and heat, it often took as much as a month or more for soldiers to become acclimated to the harsh environment. After facing the high winds that first spring and the monsoons that followed in the summer, Sam found that living in the southwest wasn't what he had imagined it would be. And it wasn't a coincidence that these troops were stationed at a fort more than forty miles from the closest town. It was common for the military to keep the colored soldiers segregated as much as possible from white townsfolk to reduce the local complaints and social objections.

For Sam, basic training wasn't a hardship; he enjoyed the comradery that made it more fun than drudgery. It didn't hurt that other Black men from Coshocton were also stationed there. At first, he thought it was a coincidence that he ended up stationed with Luther Dansby, James Woods, and Robert Taylor, all from back home. Apparently, Taylor also found it easier to go into the army than finding a job as he and the others were ordered by the judge to do. It was only later that Sam understood that all colored soldiers were restricted to a couple of regiment assignments. Stark segregation to this degree, while commonplace for most, was relatively new to him. He had grown up around

FIGURE 6.2. His first time away from home, Sam Jr. wrote to his parents often, partly to assure them that he was doing okay but also because it made him feel closer to the family he left behind.

FIGURE 6.3. Sam Jr. was a popular figure around the army base.

white folks and gone to school with them all his life even though he was often the only Black child in his classes.

Still, he planned to make the best of it. With a winning personality and natural athleticism, he quickly made friends and looked forward to trying to replicate some of his high school athletic feats by boxing and playing on the company's baseball team. Finally, he was going to benefit from the occasional lessons, willingly received or not, from his brother, Jack, who once had made quite a name for himself as a lightweight fighter in the early 1930s. He couldn't help but smile when he thought about the occasional pummeling that he took as well from his neighborhood friend Chappy, who became a professional boxer at sixteen. Those lumps that he had taken were lasting reminders of what it felt like to be whooped.

His favorite sport, by far, was baseball, where he was especially gifted on the diamond. When he slid a mitt onto his hand, it seemed to attract the ball like metal to a magnet. While standing at the plate, he squinted at the approaching ball until he felt like he could count the number of stitches on all sides. Then, he'd swing so cleanly that the bat barely made a mark when it sent the ball sailing through the gap between first and second base. It was said that he could run like the wind and often was seen carefully pulling up his knee-high socks between each stop on base. Already jack rabbit quick, he claimed it was to reduce wind drag so he could run his fastest, but it may have been his vanity at play. He always made sure to pull up those socks to hide the ugly scar on his right leg, a reminder of a close call that he'd rather forget. As claimed by the guys who teased him, his quick promotion to the rank of corporal may have resulted as much from his ability to steal bases as his performance as a soldier.

Less than a year later, his fortunes changed. Sam was making plans to return to Ohio on leave to visit his family during the winter holidays. December was especially cold that year, so he didn't relish the thought of going north later that month. Yet, he was anxious to see his family, especially his mother, Tillie Mae, with whom he was especially close despite their butting heads on occasion. After his run-in with the law from the previous summer, he was especially grateful to her for her efforts to save him from the near disaster he had faced. A letter that he sent to his parents while stationed at Fort Huachuca humbly conveyed such appreciation in verse.

MOTHER & DAD
To mother and dad whose debt I'm in
for giving me my life.
I hope I never let you down
doing my toil of strife

No one has ever gave me more
than you wonderful two
And it will take me all of my life
to ever repay or thank you

You gave me food and a place to stay
and nursed me when I was sick
Many nights I kept you awake
but neither of you would kick

Plenty of times you'd do without
The things you wanted, for me
And now I'm going to prove to you
How appreciative I can be

Now those grand old people
Are the best I've ever had
I've got God to thank for them
My mother and my dad.

Love,
Sam Jr.

He ended his letter with "May God Bless You. Leaving soon, don't write until you hear from me." There were both genuine love and gratitude fueling his desire to be with his family.

FIGURE 6.4. Tillie Sheffield was extremely proud that all of her sons served in the US military. Here, she poses with Maurice, William, and Sam Jr.

The trip home for the holidays would also be an opportunity for his older brothers to see him in uniform for the first time. Growing up, he used to sit and just stare for a long time with deep pride and admiration at the pictures of his brothers in their military uniforms, the crispness of their starched shirts and brilliance of the spit-shines on their boots. Like most boys, he imagined that one day he would serve in the army and be hailed a hero. However, it was shortly after 2 p.m. on December 7th that the first reports came streaming in and, in no time, made their way to his base. Japan had bombed the US military installations at Pearl Harbor in Hawaii. If there was any question before about whether this nation's entry into the raging war over seas could be avoided, this attack erased any doubt.

During basic training and his initial deployment, Sam was assigned to the all-Black 364th Infantry Regiment. Originally stationed in Cochise County, Arizona, the 364th was reassigned to Camp Van Dorn near Centreville, Mississippi, for retraining after alleged violent racial incidents had taken place. Maybe the army thought that bringing angry and resentful Black soldiers to the racially segregated Deep

South would help them realize how good they had it out west. As one
might have expected, the lid blew off the pot in May of 1943 when
camp guards shot a Black soldier. Before all was said and done, riots
broke out, resulting in the police firing into the crowd. Wildly diverg-
ing accounts estimated that anywhere from dozens to nearly a thousand Black soldiers were killed in what became known as the Camp
Van Dorn Massacre. As things began to cool down, the mayor of Centreville demanded that the Black troops be removed from his town.
A second near riot took place not long afterwards. By year's end, the
364th was shipped out to Alaska, where it was assigned the task of
defending key installations from the Japanese in the Aleutian Islands
for the rest of the war. What a shock, going from the sweltering Mississippi Delta to the frigid tundra.

By now a corporal, Sam was disappointed at the thought that he
might have to serve out his time in the cold northern-most region of
the country. To his surprise, things changed quickly once again. In desperate need of reinforcements, the Army decided to send along a bat-
talion from his regiment to shore up battle lines in the North Pacific.
They were relatively close by and, as some in his company suggested,
these Black soldiers might have been seen as readily expendable. They
arrived expecting the new assignment to last about six months, long
enough for the army to get its regular forces in place. They soon realized that the army had other plans when they found themselves once
again transferred to a new regiment.

It was only a matter of days before Sam was assigned to the storied
370th Infantry Regiment. Founded as a militia in the 1870s, the all-
Black 8th Infantry was re-designated the 370th and served with distinction in France during World War I. It became famous within the
Black community for the fact that it was the only unit in the whole US
army commanded entirely by colored officers. The prestige of the regiment didn't quite compare with his half-brother, Wilson's, service with
the 477th Bombardment Group of the US Army Air Force, known
more commonly as the Tuskegee Airmen. Still, there was no sense
chasing after his older brother's laurels when he should be out to earn
his own. Wild speculation about where they might go was rampant.

Would they go to the Philippines? Maybe they would head to France or Italy.

Consistent with the practice of segregation within the military, Sam's stint in the army, regardless of his assignment, was one where he found himself surrounded by faces the same color as his. Growing up in rural Ohio, his only experience being in the presence of large numbers of only his own people took place at church camp meetings or on Sundays at his father's church. Several of the younger guys just arriving at the base that he came to know talked often about wanting to see some action. Some even predicted that they were sure to be decorated for bravery in battle. This kind of talk went on for what seemed like forever since the three hundred and seventieth spent nearly two years training before it departed the United States. Given that Sam had already spent time in the Asia Pacific Theatre, he was immediately popular as one of the few who had actually seen some action. When the time came to move out, there was a great deal of secrecy about their assignment. Where the regiment was being sent wasn't clear; they weren't told even after they were lined up on the pier, herded aboard a transport ship, and were several miles out to sea.

Before his assignment in the North Pacific, Sam had never been on a ship before, especially one bigger than anything else he'd ever seen in his life. Now, for the second time, he would find himself at sea. He used to dream that one day he would travel, but those dreams didn't include being squeezed into the hull of a ship with thousands of anxious men, many of whom were often disgustingly nauseous during the voyage. Just as being stationed in the Asia Pacific didn't turn out to be like living in a tropical paradise, he knew that moving on to the next military outpost in the islands or elsewhere would likely bring more of the same. But, he just wanted to survive the voyage for a second time.

Prior to going to the service, Sam had only heard of sea sickness, but nothing prepared him for what he witnessed daily on these trips. The noise and smell were, at times, overwhelming. He had come from a rural environment that was filled with endless fresh air and was quiet enough for him to make out the distinctive sounds of each type of bird that occasionally roosted in the fruit trees on the edge of their property.

The air that he encountered in the bunks at night was always stale, and during the days when it was his turn to go up top, the salty wind left his nostrils caked with thick deposits. He swore that he'd never complain again about the black plumes that belched out from the smokestacks of the factories back home or curse when the trains that traveled the railroad tracks near his home would let out a sharp whistle.

By now, those things that Sam once viewed as major annoyances would be welcome in an instant compared to the assaults upon his senses during that voyage. The only thing vaguely familiar during these journeys was the night sky. As the vessel pushed forward after dark, it moved under orders of low lights, sometimes no lights. This was to reduce the chances of their transport ships being targeted by the enemy during random attacks at night. While his city-born companions marveled at the night's foreboding darkness during cloud-covered evenings, followed on subsequent nights by the brilliance of starlit constellations, he was used to late evening vistas that bore witness to the infinite immenseness of the universe, unencumbered by manmade skylines and streetlights. He smiled as he recalled his mother, renowned singer and evangelist that she was, belting out one of his favorite verses, "It took a miracle to hang the world in space . . ."

Speculation and rumors soon took center stage. Word quickly spread that they would be landing soon. When the 370th arrived at its destination, the seriousness of war became readily apparent to the disembarking men when they discovered that the hordes of men standing on the pier were not there to welcome them but to be transported to hospitals back home to treat the many injuries both plainly visible as they passed by as well as those lodged deeply inside of them like enemy bullets that found their mark. Whether they were likely to face fighting or not, Sam was just grateful to get back onto solid ground. Even though the colored troops to which he was attached only had primary responsibility for logistical support, he felt as though he had already seen more than he cared to see of what the ravages of war could do.

Young boys, no older than he was, came back from the front lines irreversibly changed, some returning without limbs and others bringing back with them the horror of seeing death all around them. In some ways, seeing them made him feel that his job of supplying the frontline guys with munitions, supplies, and rations was much more important than he had originally thought. Without the hard work of his regiment, the men being shot at would have stood no chance. And, having grown up out in the country, he was no stranger to hard work. His industriousness quickly led to another promotion; he found himself with a few more stripes sewn onto his uniform. He liked the sound of it when the enlisted men called him master sergeant. As the war wound down, Sam finished his tour of duty and headed home in early November of 1945. Of his nearly five years in the army, he had spent two and a half of those in the Asiatic Pacific Theatre and a few months near the end in Italy. By the end of the month, he arrived back in Coshocton.

Service in the military can change young men . . . forever. It doesn't matter whether you saw combat or not, just being in the army makes you grow up fast. You will see things and do things that you've never seen or done before. When you return home, you will have changed, oftentimes in ways that family and friends may not fully understand or appreciate. If Sam Jr. thought that his hometown was boring and lifeless when he left at eighteen, it was worse, if that could be possible, when he returned. The same people, the same work, when work was even available, and the same old deafening quiet that has a way of sucking the life right out of you. He had never scared easily, but now his greatest fear was that he would end up living out his life in this god-forsaken backwater of a town doing whatever the generations of colored men had been limited to doing throughout their time in this predominantly white, rural community. If he had left a boy, he definitely came back a man. In some ways, he came back a Black man, even if he didn't fully understand or appreciate it at the time how much his treatment by the legal system shaped his view of injustices targeted against men whose skin was the same color as his. After serving in a segregated regiment in the South where he witnessed firsthand the indignities and violence against men who looked like he did, life could never be the same for him.

CHAPTER 7

READING, WRITING, AND 'RITHMETIC

Over in neighboring Mt. Vernon, everything about life on Miami Street seemed so fresh and new to Oneida, from the time she finally joined her mother and her new stepfather. As she later reminded me, Lon was the only true father that she'd ever had. The sun shined brighter; the air smelled fresher. Even the chicken pens did not make her turn up her nose like she had done on Grandpa's farm. She occasionally was asked to feed the chickens and preferred that to collecting the eggs. She didn't like being pecked, constantly worrying about their flapping wings when she stuck her hand into the nests to feel around for the warm ovals. Her favorite household chore, though, was delivering the eggs to customers around the neighborhood. Propping her small, red Murray bicycle against the rain barrel at the corner of the house, she'd ladle water into a white porcelain bowl and wash each egg one by one while arranging them according to their sizes. She'd carefully load them into the basket on her bike, separating the cardboard containers with wadded-up newspaper to minimize the jostling. Then, she'd jump on and pedal quickly down the street with her mother calling sharply behind that she'd better slow down else she'd end up delivering cracked eggs. Cracked eggs were bad for business since they could only sell them for half price—if the cracks weren't all that bad—or, worse, give them away free if the egg whites were seeping through.

While being responsible and doing her chores was important to Lon and Bertha, it was Oneida's schooling that they emphasized time and time again. Despite the persistent call in Black America that educational advancement was the key to racial equality, formal schooling wasn't a high priority for colored subsistence farmers in those days. Most felt that lifting up the race through education would have to be left to reformers like Booker T. Washington. Poor colored farmers depended upon their ability to raise chickens and livestock or tend crops to get by, not so much reading, writing, and arithmetic, although being good with numbers did come in handy at times. That was what was seen for generations in both families. For example, by the age of eleven, Bertha's father, June, had already stopped attending school even though he could not yet read or write. It was for his family's well-being that he was needed as a laborer on the Edwards' farm. Just as his older brothers, William, Charles, and John, had done, he left school to help out on the farm. He felt sorry for his nine-year-old brother, Coulson, who would be expected to do the same, never having a chance to maybe make more for his life.

Bertha couldn't help but wonder what her life would have been like if she had had the chance to finish her schooling or, for that matter, just to experience what she could only imagine to be a typical child's life. Instead, much of her latter childhood was spent having daily responsibility for her three younger siblings as well as having to fend for herself. Although her formal education never advanced beyond the sixth grade, she showed more smarts in the way she helped her father manage their household than an adult with a business college degree ordinarily does. She was especially proud when her youngest daughter, Oneida, finished high school. In some ways, she shared in that graduation as if it was partly her own. While her book smarts may have been limited, her natural talent with numbers and measurements enabled her to take care of most of the bill paying chores for her father. That ability stayed with her after being twice widowed and long into old age. She was so proud that local merchants were willing to extend her credit, even on the meager income that a maid could earn. From the Community Market, where Mrs. Starmer allowed her to run a tab, to the downtown Montgomery Ward department store, where she purchased her first gas-powered lawn mower, she made sure that she never missed a payment nor was she ever late. She often told her daughters that "being on time with your payments was being late," so she made it a habit to pay her bills as soon as they arrived regardless of the due dates. Her bills were always paid as many days before they were due as she could possibly manage and usually by money order since she didn't have a checking account.

Oneida soaked it all up. Without her mother ever saying it directly, she knew how disappointed Bertha was that her other girls didn't finish school. Knowing that Ina Mae only made it to the sixth grade and Mary Jane to the eighth, my mother was determined to be the first to graduate from high school. Attending the elementary school just a few blocks away was a good start. She was an eager learner with a politeness that made her a teacher's favorite. The feelings were mutual as she quickly bonded with her teachers year after year. Lonnie would have expected nothing less from her. The first thing out of his mouth after getting home from work was, "Neet, got your homework done?" He was quick to sit down with her and listen to her recitations or help her practice her spelling words.

While Lon himself only made it through the sixth grade, he felt it was his job to keep Oneida focused on her studies. Something about the girl told him that she had the makings of something special. And, he knew that it would take her believing in herself. He was intent on modeling an inquisitive mind, spending an hour pouring over the newspaper before reaching into his dark walnut bookcase with the framed glass openings to pick out one of the history books that he had collected. On occasion, he would pull down the Paul Lawrence Dunbar poetry book that he had gotten from his brother, George, and read a stanza or two out loud in his booming baritone voice. He insisted that she learn and always speak "proper English," never hesitating to gently correct her if he heard her misspeak. "You never know when someone important will hear you and make decisions about you that will last a lifetime . . . and you know white folks expect you to get it wrong, anyways. Don't be like most colored folks, always trying to 'toe the line.'

FIGURE 7.1. Witnessing Oneida graduate from high school brought
Bertha much joy and fulfilled one of her grandest wishes.

Get my meaning, girl? Can't let no color line hold you back. You and I
both know that you have it in you to be better than that."

It wasn't long before Oneida started junior high school in the
recently erected Mulberry Street school building that brought together
children in grades seven through twelve from across the town. While
the expanse of the building and the hordes of young people were a bit
intimidating for a reserved adolescent girl, she was, at the same time,
excited about regularly seeing other children who looked like her. After

spending a few years in an elementary school where she was often one of only two, sometimes three, colored children in the entire school, she found herself having more frequent encounters with the kids who she would not otherwise have seen except on Sunday mornings at church when what seemed like the entire colored community would gather. A combination of being in a new school and her natural shyness made her gravitate to activities where she didn't feel as though she stuck out. Having nurtured a love for reading, she found herself visiting the school library on every occasion that she could. Mrs. Sevitts, the librarian, took notice of this small, quiet girl who immersed herself in a wide range of fantastical tales. Growing up in a family and station in life where such things were often beyond their means, she never had a chance to travel or engage in other costly leisure. For her, reading was the next best thing. She was drawn to stories that took her, by way of a very active imagination, to lands far away.

Helen Sevitts was unique by every measure, and not just as far as rural high school librarians go. Mrs. Sevitts had earned her college degree from Western Reserve University in Cleveland and graduate degrees, including a doctorate, from Columbia University and the College of Wooster. She brought to the Mt. Vernon schools a worldliness and sophistication not often seen among the educational staffs in small towns. Whether she had been accustomed to more racial diversity than most or, like some liberal whites, felt a special calling to reach out to this quiet colored girl, she was often seen speaking softly to Oneida, her words interspersed with an occasional chuckle. By the end of the next year, Mrs. Sevitts encouraged her to join the high school library staff.

Slowly, Oneida began to feel more comfortable and joined her first club, Girls Reserves. The Girls Reserves was ostensibly a rural debutante's service club, but it looked more like a launching pad for homecoming courts and eventual appearances in the town newspaper's society pages. She couldn't recall who convinced her to join, or why, but she soon realized that several of its members were the daughters of women for whom her mother and sisters had worked as maids. When she discovered later on that the club's big event each year was a mother-daughter banquet, she fretted about how that might go. Eventually, she concocted a flimsy excuse that she gave to the girls about how she would have to drop out because of responsibilities she had at home. It wasn't that she was ashamed of her mother's occupation as a maid. To the contrary, she was extremely proud of her, especially how she managed to survive and provide for her family beginning at an early age, persevering through the kind of personal tragedies that would have broken the spirit of most people. Most importantly for Oneida, she wanted to spare her mother the indignities of having those other moms looking down their noses at her mother. Just the thought that some snobbish white woman might insult her mother or make her feel unwelcome brought tears to her eyes. Besides, she knew that Bertha was more comfortable with her hands deep in dirt in the yard and or in a bucket of soapy water while scrubbing floors around the house than wearing white gloves and making small talk with women who probably never had to work a day in their lives.

When her sophomore year arrived, Oneida tried athletics, participating in intramural basketball and volleyball. Always somewhat of a tomboy as she toiled around the farm, she thought she'd give it a whirl. She was motivated, in part, by a chance encounter with an owl. That poor old owl had the misfortune of taking up residence in the tree outside her window and screeched like the dickens all night long. As she recalled it, she couldn't take it any longer, so she and her mother went outside to put a stop to it. Bertha showed her how to find just the right kind of stone and demonstrated how to rid her yard of the pest. Calling upon every ounce of strength that her five-foot-two-inch frame could muster, Oneida's mother picked up a perfectly flat rock and hurled it with all her might toward the owl. To both of their surprise, the owl fell out of the tree and, after unceremoniously bouncing on its head, got up and flew away never to be seen, or more importantly, heard again in the tree outside her window. Unfortunately, her mother's accuracy with rocks wasn't passed on to Oneida, and her diminutive size and lack of competitiveness did not lead to success in sports. She usually was reluctant to ever try to score even a single point during the games. The more aggressive girls on her teams liked that she was all too willing to give them the ball along with the opportunities that she gladly passed up. So, her cautious and reluctant experiment with school sports didn't last very long.

Still, Oneida's confidence in school grew with the encouragement of Mrs. Sevitts, her role model and the one adult at her school who had taken her under her wing and was her main booster. Oneida even summoned up the courage to participate in a theatrical production, *Harvest Harmonies,* if only in a bit role. That was fine with her that she didn't have a featured part; she didn't need or seek the limelight and would have been happy to go unnoticed altogether. Little did she realize that this would not be the only time in her life that she would find herself upon a stage or drawing admiring attention from a large audience.

Working in the school library was far and away Oneida's favorite activity. After only two years of participation on the staff, she was made president during her junior year, an honor usually bestowed upon a senior. Whether her selection came after a vote by the other students on the staff or was the result of an appointment by the supportive librarian, she always credited Mrs. Sevitts with giving her the confidence to excel as a member of the library staff. During my youth, our family couldn't afford the usual recreational activities that others seemed to enjoy. That didn't deter my mother from trying to create fun outings for us. From her many pleasant hours communing with the books, she knew that a visit to the library was free. So, she took her children to the local public library nearly every week, sometimes walking clear across town, delighting all the while in telling us about the Dewey decimal catalog system. Politely listening to her explain how it worked, we didn't let on that we didn't understand any of it nor were we the least bit interested. But she clearly was, so we were happy to watch her eyes light up as she talked about her days working at the library.

She'd sit at the library's low children's table with us, contorting her body so that she could get her legs and knees underneath it, and softly read us books aloud. She did this week after week until we acquired the ability to read them for ourselves. I was excited when the day came that I finally got my own peach-colored library card containing a tiny metal plate with an embossed number and my name printed in blue ink. I

took enormous pride in walking to the desk and handing the
attendant my limit of two books
that I wanted to take home.
Then, I'd offer her my own personal library card that I knew
vouched for my being responsible enough to take good care
of the materials placed in my
charge. My mother's passion for
books, and reading to children
especially, remained with her

FIGURE 7.2. It was Oneida's job in the school library
that made her feel most at home.

throughout her life, her voice modulating with the change of characters
as she read to my own children. Well into her eighties, she would often
recall with great fondness her high school librarian. It wasn't until I
was in my sixties, rummaging through some files, that I discovered a
signature on the guest book of my father's funeral service. Written in
a compassionate, reassuring script was the name "Mrs. Helen Sevitts."

Determined not to follow in her mother's and sisters' footsteps by
settling for day work as just another of the many colored maids in
Mt. Vernon, Oneida wanted more out of life. In addition to the confidence boost that the library job had been for her, the managers of the
local department store approached her about working there. Of course,
they didn't have anyone of her race working as a salesperson or behind
the display counter, but they thought that with her pleasant smile and
friendly disposition that she would make an excellent elevator operator.
So, she hired on during the summer running the elevator for customers
at Rudin's, one of only two department stores in all of the downtown.
Ironically, she ended up replacing Mr. Lee, the longtime janitor and
elevator operator. Art Lee, a relative newcomer to the local Black community, married Stella White, whose brother, Stanley, would become
the future husband of Oneida's sister, Mary Jane. Art and Stella would
eventually buy a house and live directly across the street from my family. Perhaps Oneida's hire was not as much of a coincidence as originally thought given that it just so happened that her mother, Bertha,

worked as a maid for the Rudin family. She would often recall going with her mother to the stately Rudin home on East Gambier Street and sitting patiently in the backyard waiting for her mother to finish her day's work. Sometimes, she would head downtown from school to meet her mother at the Rudins' house for that long walk home. Bertha, like many women of her generation, never learned to drive. So, she was in the habit of walking to work or to do the shopping, pulling her cart briskly behind her. So, Oneida's patience and politeness often shined through. Apparently, the owners were impressed by this pretty, well-behaved little girl. So, when she got older, they arranged for her to become the first colored female employee to work at the store.

Inspired by a couple of older Black women in the community who had once attended Mt. Vernon Business College, the local vocational school for aspiring secretaries, Oneida enrolled there to hone her typing and dictation skills. She was often told that with her good looks and solid secretarial skills, she would be a shoo-in for snagging one of those jobs. The only problem was, there weren't any colored girls working as secretaries in her town. It soon became clear that in order for her to land a job as a secretary she would have to go elsewhere. She initially thought she'd look for work in Columbus, but the big city frightened her a bit. She had a couple of unpleasant run-ins with some eastside neighborhood roughs when she went there to visit her longtime friend Suzie. On more than one occasion, Sue found herself stepping between her country friend and some sassy girl who was more than happy to "permanently slap that lovely smile off" Oneida's face. They would accuse her of thinking she was cute because she had light skin and good hair. Though both of her grandmothers were white, she never talked about that since it seemed to be a sore point among the Black girls she met. Sue made sure to never leave her friend's side when she came to visit because she knew that those tough girls meant business. It wasn't unheard of at the time for pretty young girls and women to be scarred or disfigured by having caustic lye thrown into their faces. It didn't take long for Oneida to conclude that maybe she just wasn't ready yet for the big city.

CHAPTER 8

MISS BRONZE OHIO

Everybody knows that young folks need some excitement in their lives. Oneida was no different, so she didn't hesitate in the summer of 1946 when Stanley White, a former local high school star athlete a few years her senior and future brother-in-law, offered to take her for a ride on his motorcycle. He told her that it would be a quick ride to the store to get a pack of cigarettes. Once they sped past the community market, it quickly became clear that the journey would not be as brief or short as he had claimed. Heading east and riding at nearly top speed over the hills and along the curvy roads, they arrived in Coshocton in a matter of no time. She hadn't spent much time in that town, her place of birth, since she left it for Mt. Vernon around the time she was beginning primary school. It was on this spur of the moment excursion that she met a good-looking young man who took a keen interest in her. By chance, Oneida happened to meet young Sam Sheffield Jr., a handsome and charming guy who almost instantly swept her off her feet. She didn't have a lot of experience dating, having grown up under the watchful and protective eye of her stepfather. Lonnie made it clear that he wasn't having any of those fast city boys in their flashy zoot suits with garish chains falling out of their oversized pockets coming around his home. Sam didn't talk or act like a city guy. Even though he was six years older and had served in the military, he didn't seem to her all

that much different than the boys with whom she had grown up and
gone to high school. Clearly forgetting that she was supposed to feign
disinterest and play hard to get, it was quickly apparent that Oneida
was immediately smitten. While she didn't want to admit it to herself,
she rode back to Mt. Vernon certain that she had met the man that she
would marry. Working hard against acting upon that gut impulse was
her promise to herself that she would at least try to make a go of it as a
secretary before settling down to get married and have children.

As a teen, the slow pace and relative friendliness of small-town living was what Oneida had become most accustomed to experiencing in
her young life. As much as she fantasized about the allure of the bright
lights and sounds, she found in her rural environs a refuge from the
harshness that many in her family, her sisters especially, had endured
in their lives. Now, as a young woman, she still wanted to spread her
wings and yearned for more in life than what she was receiving in Mt.
Vernon. Most of the other colored girls her age were already married
or pregnant, and only sometimes both. By the spring of '47, she found
herself being recruited to enter a statewide pageant by the older sister
of her friend and high school classmate Peggy Sharp. Ruth Sharp was
a stringer for the Columbus colored newspaper, the *Ohio State News.*
The *News* was the primary sponsor of the Miss Bronze Ohio pageant,
a noted beauty competition that, as the name indicates, was held for
comely Black women around the state who otherwise were not permitted to compete in the Miss Ohio and other pageants open only
to white women. While she was flattered, it was going to be a hard
sell to get this reserved girl to agree. But Ruth had a way of making it
seem not so threatening. With promises of "loads of fun" and mutual
support, plans began to take shape. Before long, she had convinced six
local girls to join herself and her four sisters as contestants. Having
eleven Black girls from little Mt. Vernon, Ohio, among the more than
one hundred statewide was rather remarkable. Perhaps more surprising
to those who knew her was that Oneida Fisher was among them.

Oneida's pageant experience, as she later recalled, was among the
highlights of her life, even sixty years later. It also involved one of the
most direct competitions between her older sister Mary Jane and her-

self. Her sister was what many called "a real beauty." And, Mary Jane, from an early age, loved the adoration and attention, at least most of the time. Unfortunately, much of that attention came from grown men who frequently offered her a nickel if she'd come and sit on their laps. When my mother was much older, she expressed a sadness about how her sister's striking good looks turned out to be more of a curse than an asset. My mother attributed Mary Jane's early teen pregnancies to her being all too willing to sit ("and who knew what else") for those nickels. And having two children before she reached 18 did not squelch her hunger for such attention. Her first marriage at barely16 to a man more than a dozen years her senior saved her from living the life of the proverbial unwed mother.

Following the birth of her second child, a son, Mary Jane moved to Columbus for less than a year before that marriage fell apart. Shortly thereafter, she returned to Mt. Vernon, but taking up residence again with Bertha and Lon didn't last long. Within a couple months, she accepted a marriage proposal from a divorcee, Lester Martin, a man who was sixteen years older than her and who married for the first time only a year after his new wife-to-be was even born. But, all that seemed to matter to Mary Jane at the time was that she got out of a bad, loveless marriage and, with two children in tow, could quickly enter another one regardless of the man's age. My mother always wondered if her sister even loved Lester or if she had only agreed to marry him simply to get out from under the strict rules that her mother and Lonnie imposed upon her. Her parents had made it clear to Mary Jane that as a condition of her moving in that they wouldn't put up with the type of carousing and gallivanting that apparently had become her practice. They were not going to have it, not under their roof. There were to be no more mouths to feed at 8 Miami Street because of her catting around.

When Ruth Sharp began to recruit colored girls throughout Mt. Vernon to compete in the Miss Bronze Ohio pageant, Mary Jane did not come to her mind because the contestants were not supposed to be married or have been previously married. Mary Jane was both, and she wasn't the least bit hesitant to omit those facts when she submitted her application. This pageant would be precisely the type of attention that she'd always sought, some validation that she was, in fact, the fairest of all. She'd be admired by men and women, even those jealous of her stunning good looks. She was sure that others would sit up and take notice of her beauty. So, no convincing her to enter the contest was necessary. From the outset, all of the contestants were expected to obtain commercial sponsors who would pay the entry fees and expenses that the young women would incur to participate. Photographs of the contestants were required at the time of application and, despite objections from Oneida's mother, Lonnie paid for the photo session. "Oh, Bert, give the girl a chance." His confidence and investment in her apparently paid off.

Sitting in the *News'* conference room where stacks of photographs of pretty girls laid strewn around the table, Oneida, like all of the other contestants, was interviewed by the pageant staff. They were already convinced that she was what they called "a looker," but it was her apparent shyness and modesty that sealed the deal. Oneida became the first girl from Mt. Vernon to get a pageant sponsor when the Club Regal contacted her to represent them in the competition. Club Regal, situated directly across the street from the popular Lincoln Theatre on Long Street, was widely regarded as "one of the classiest joints" on Columbus' Black east side. Frequented by the city's Black businessmen and professionals, it was not unusual to spot a doctor or lawyer there as well as entertainers who were performing or just passing through Columbus. Oneida had been there at least once before, and her presence did not go unnoticed. In fact, in the end, she and her friend Peggy were the only local girls to have sponsors. In explaining Mary Jane's rejection by potential sponsors, my mother thought that it was a combination of her sister's deception and her vanity that kept them away. She felt that they all acknowledged that Mary Jane had the looks, but Oneida felt that her sister didn't win over people because they saw her as sassy and conceited. It was only after many years had passed that my mother began to believe that much of what people were seeing was all an act on Mary Jane's part to try to appear confident when she had suffered from feeling bad about herself for most of her life.

Leading up to the summer pageant, Oneida was mentioned in the *Ohio State News* as one of the favorites. Her sponsorship may have played a major role in her emerging as a potential top pick. Club Regal, owned by one of the best known of the city's handful of Black attorneys, was thought to have considerable influence with the pageant's sponsor, *Ohio State News*. The advertising revenue generated by both the nightclub and the law practice was nothing to overlook, but it was the advantage gained when such customers and clients were regularly referred to the paper that made a difference. It also didn't hurt that my mother felt that she had a very positive interview with the pageant's judges. With her usual humble demeanor, she expressed her gratitude in those meetings "for just being invited to compete with all those attractive and talented girls." She assured the judges that it would be an experience that she'd never forget, especially coming from such a small town.

By early summer, her courtship with that handsome man from Coshocton, Sam Sheffield, was becoming more serious. He made it clear to her, however, that he was not the least bit pleased that she had become a contestant. It had less to do with the fact that he was the son of a Baptist preacher and knew that his parents would disapprove of her being in a pageant than his dislike of having all of those men ogling and leering at her, thinking who knows what thoughts about her. He told her that if she went through with it he wouldn't come to support her. In fact, she may as well consider them done. It was too late for her to back out. She had promised her friends that she would participate, and she would live up to her word even if it led to the breakup of her relationship with Sam.

By the end of the second day of the contest, it was clear that Oneida was right. She surely would not forget "just being in the pageant." To do so would have required her to forget as well that she became a finalist and eventually finished fourth overall in the statewide competition. For years, members of Mt. Vernon's Black community proudly, although inaccurately, claimed that she had won the pageant. That mistaken belief of her victory troubled her since folks seemed to forget that her friend Irene Sharp had done even better, finishing ahead of

FIGURE 8.1. Oneida Fisher poses in her Miss Bronze Ohio contestant apparel during the 1947 pageant run by the *Ohio State News*, a Black-owned and operated Columbus newspaper of the time.

her in second place while her sister Ruth Sharp ended up tenth. Folks rarely mentioned that, some thinking that Ruth took advantage of her position as a writer for the *Ohio State News* and that allowed her sister and her to advance so far in the competition.

Oneida's most vivid memory of the event was not how well she did but looking out into the audience and seeing "Sammy" present. As much as he wanted to, he couldn't suppress his beaming smile, although later he denied having smiled at all. If he did, he said, it probably must have been because some attractive girl in the audience asked him who he was. Whether he was willing to admit it or not, he wasn't the only one proud of her. As much as it appeared so out of place among the staid photographs adorning the walls of her parents' living room, there hung a color photo of Oneida in a two-piece bathing suit. On loan to her by her pageant sponsor, Club Regal, the revealing outfit was adorned with a sash that proudly claimed the club's relationship with this young beauty from a small town north of the city. There hung that photo for all to see, even the little old ladies who come to the house for the missionary society meetings that my grandmother hosted on occasion.

The summer of 1947 was eventful enough with the pageant alone, but there was no time to waste. If she was going to make her break from her hometown, especially after Sam's ultimatum, then she needed to make up her mind. After talking it over with her mother, Oneida decided to go live with her sister Ina and her second husband, John Fredericks, in Welch, West Virginia. Welch, the county seat of McDowell County, was smaller than Mt. Vernon, and certainly didn't resemble what anyone would consider a city. It did, though, have a sizeable colored community with nearly twenty percent of the inhabitants being Black. Like many towns in that region, it was once a part of the state of Virginia and struggled, continuing to this day, to come to terms with its long history of chattel slavery. After emancipation, Black families remained there to take up some of the dirty, backbreaking jobs available to them in the coalmines. They stayed even though, like most towns and cities south of the Ohio River, it followed the rigid rules of segregation closely. Still, within days, she managed to get an interview and was hired on the spot as a receptionist and secretary for the area's only Black lawyer, Stewart A. Calhoun.

FIGURE 8.2. Oneida Fisher and Sam Sheffield
Jr. in the early days of their courtship.

Lawyer Calhoun, as Oneida called him, grew up in one of the most prosperous colored families in the area. His father was the proprietor of the largest saloon in Keystone, managing to keep his businesses going, first as a speakeasy during Prohibition, then a popular juke joint to drown one's sorrows during the Depression, and later a family restaurant. A light-skinned man with perfectly coifed straight hair, he struck what many said was quite a handsome figure with looks that some credited for the business and social standing that few others in his community had attained. Having inherited his father's good looks and dapper style, it was no surprise that Stewart quickly established himself early in his career.

Of course, there were also Stewart's father's connections that seemed to go back a couple of generations due to his uncanny ability to somehow manage to get his hands on the right libations to lubricate club events and private parties that were attended in those days by the town's well-heeled and local office holders. Even the sheriff and district attorney could be spotted there from time to time, just "keeping the peace." Upon my prompting, Oneida enjoyed describing her work as a legal secretary, perhaps as a way of connecting it with the fact that her son had grown up to become a lawyer. She admitted, though, that she didn't recall ever seeing Black people come into Mr. Calhoun's Keystone office where she frequently worked. Well, unless you count her brother-in-law, who on occasion would stop by the office purportedly to keep an eye on her, only, of course, after having had a few beers. He said he knew that shady characters frequented law offices, and it was his duty as her sister's husband to make sure she was safe. She found it all embarrassing, and it was clear to her that John seemed to get a kick out of bragging to his drinking buddies about her fancy job with this local big shot lawyer as well as the looks he got when he occasionally dropped in on her at work.

CHAPTER 9

SAYING "I DO"
AND THEN DOING IT

Shortly after launching her career as a secretary in the adjoining state, Oneida began to get letters and increasingly insistent long-distance phone calls from what she tried to convince herself was by now a former love interest, Sam Sheffield. She said that Sam told her that it was time for them to stop pretending that they weren't made to be together. He told her that he would be driving the six hours to West Virginia after work that Friday so that they could talk things out. Talk things out they did because by the end of August a wedding date was set. Sam and Oneida made plans to be wed on the sprawling lawn at 8 Miami Street. The following month, the two were married in a gorgeous display of floral splendor. Finally, Lonnie got to see his majestic manor host an event that featured one of his own. Sam and Oneida didn't disappoint; they actually looked the part of small-town colored royalty. It was if they had stepped right off the cover of that new race magazine, *Ebony*; for their families, there could not have been a more beautiful couple.

The couple immediately began to build a modest home on a parcel of land given to them by Lon and Bertha, little more than a half-acre or so away on the edge of her parents' property. With the help of Sam's father, a skilled bricklayer and carpenter, they quickly dug out a foundation and erected the frame. Whether Sammy thought she was

FIGURE 9.1. Oneida Fisher weds Sam Sheffield Jr. at the home of her parents, Lon and Bertha Hammonds.

FIGURE 9.2. Often told they were made for each other, Oneida and Sam found that the early years of marriage seemed to meet all their expectations of wedded bliss.

FIGURE 9.3. Sam Jr. and his father begin immediately building
the modest house that he and his new bride would occupy.

being silly or not, Oneida insisted on placing handwritten notes in the
cornerstone blocks, hers professing eternal love for her husband. She
never found out what his note said since he refused to share it with her
even after she read her note aloud to him first. Together, they carefully
folded the notes and placed them in the jar that they gently set in the
foundation block. Before long, their new home rose from the ground.
Sam immediately christened the home with the name "2nd Heaven,"
which he carefully carved into a board and nailed it to the tree in the
front of the house. In order to avoid having to cut the tree down as
they were finishing the house, he poured the front sidewalk into a Y
shape that led directly to the front porch.

The house was a perfect fit for just the two of them as it neared
completion in early November. The kitchen, bathroom, and a single
bedroom adjoined the larger room that would serve as their combination living room and dining room area. At one end was the fireplace, the scene of many joyous holidays to come, even though she
insisted that the measurements for the mantle were off by nearly a

FIGURE 9.4. Oneida and Sam Jr.'s modest new house is erected
just a stone's throw from Oneida's parents' home.

foot. Oneida claimed responsibility for the mismeasurement, eventually deciding the off-center fireplace gave their home some special character. At the other end sat a dark brown gas stove with a grate that glowed orangish-yellow when called upon to provide warmth for the occupants. Years later, she would chuckle about how her children would lie in a line, one pressed tightly against the other, in front of that old stove to get warm, frequently adjusting their positions when the one in the front got too hot and the one farthest away too cold. Just to the right of where the stove sat was a pass-through between the kitchen and dining area that Sam proudly claimed would prove to be a step-saver for his bride. It turned out that before long she was going to need that extra help. As winter arrived, Oneida discovered that she was pregnant with her first child. Excited but somewhat afraid, she increasingly felt for the first time what for her became a pattern of acute sickness and discomfort when she was expecting. The newness of the sensations stirring in her belly left her constantly worried if things were all right. The answer came about six weeks later when she woke up with a start. She had no experience to draw upon but her instincts told her that something was terribly wrong. And the evidence on her sheet and a subsequent call to fetch a doctor confirmed that she had lost the baby.

Like many new brides who failed to complete a first-time pregnancy, Oneida wondered if she had done something wrong or was one of those women destined to be childless. Despite assurances from her mother as well as her older sister Ina, who had experienced miscarriages before, Oneida worried about whether she would ever get pregnant again and if she could carry a child to term. That worry about future infertility ended after another bout of sickness that next fall, confirming both that she was with child and that this would be another difficult pregnancy. By this time, Lon had been successful in getting Sam a job at the glass factory where he himself was employed. With the full responsibility of maintaining the young couple's household while her husband was away, Oneida was determined that she would clean her house, do the laundry, and make dinner for Sam when he got home in the evenings. She had watched her mother do all of this and more for her entire life, and she wanted to follow in those footsteps. Looking at her daughter's tiny frame and the constant nausea, Bertha made it a point each day to walk over to her house and check on her. While there, she just so happened to find herself helping with whatever household chores needed done.

While the months passed, Oneida's constant sickness and discomfort began to lessen or perhaps she didn't notice it quite so much. Spring arrived and passed quickly as she awaited the expansion of her family, hopefully accompanied by a shrinking of what to her felt like an enormous stomach. In almost no time, what emerged from her was a beautiful baby boy. She had always thought that Sammy would want to name his first son after himself and his father, but her husband quickly dispelled that thought when he told her that he had learned early in his life that one Sam Sheffield in the house was plenty. Two Sams, he assured her, could sometimes be a handful for any sane woman. Just ask his mother, Tillie. Out of fondness toward one of his service buddies, his first born would be named Gregg, a

FIGURE 9.5. Sam Jr., with his beaming smile, relishes the
role of being a new father with his firstborn son.

mighty good first name for a son, he thought, and distinctive in that it would be spelled with two "g's."

Her initial self-doubts to the contrary, Oneida quickly showed that she was a natural when it came to being a loving and caring mother. Her attentiveness to her newborn was matched only by Sam's penchant for bragging about his son. Maybe, it was as much bragging about himself, since he'd tell anyone who'd listen that it took a special kind of man to sire a son. Oneida was sure that he had rehearsed that line, probably borrowed from his dad, Sam Sr., along with another one that he had practiced had the child she delivered been a girl. It wasn't long before she would find out as that oh-too-familiar queasiness beset her once again. Eight months after the birth of Gregg, she realized that something was once again stirring inside of her. On November 22nd of that year, she gave birth to their daughter Karen. Sam reveled in hearing from friends and family how his children had to be the most beautiful ever born. And the cycle continued with the discovery six months later that she was pregnant once more, this time suffering the same fate as befell her during the first one. She would have had a second son. Again, any renewed worries she had about fertility were for naught; she became pregnant again within a few months. In July, just a couple of months short of their sixth anniversary, Oneida gave birth to a second daughter, Debra. Holding her up high upon his chest to be seen by his parents who had traveled from Coshocton to see the newest Sheffield, Sam beamed the way that only fathers can when they have been blessed by what he liked to call his perfect children. By now with three, Sam was saying that he'd be damned if he and his wife would stop at an odd number. That could be bad luck. It seemed that before his words had even stopped reverberating in the wind, she discovered once more that God must have had a plan for her body, even if she wasn't so sure if she agreed with it. One thing was for sure; she certainly couldn't entertain even the thought that he might want her to match his mother's feat of giving birth to eleven!

It became apparent that the little house on Miami Street could no longer comfortably hold this growing family. Sam enlisted the aid of his father to begin building on a couple of additional bedrooms. He thought that with the increase in the size of his family his four kids should share two of the rooms: the boys in one and the girls in the other. He and his wife should have their own. Besides, as things became more crowded, his hope for some privacy seemed to fade. The following summer, Oneida gave birth to their second son, Ricci, naming me after another friend from Sam's time in the service. Perhaps the name reminded him as well of the time he spent angling to get stationed in Italy during the war. When she brought him home from the hospital, the

FIGURE 9.6. Sam Jr. and Oneida's family has grown after the birth of their third child.

lone, small bedroom that the whole family shared was outfitted with two twin-sized wooden bunk beds. In one, mother and newborn slept down below with the oldest child overhead. In the other bed, the toddler slept with her father with older sister up on top. The parents must have found occasions to put the infant and toddler in the same bed since in about six months she was expecting a fifth child. But, as had been her misfortune twice before, she was unable to carry the little girl to term.

It wasn't just the size of the family that was changing, but their financial security or lack thereof. Not long after the birth of their youngest, Sam's health unexpectedly and dramatically declined. While working at the glass factory, he suffered some sort of spell and fell headlong into one of the conveyor belts. A few steps farther and it might have been onto a furnace. Lamb Glass Company, concerned about potential liability and trouble with the agency overseeing occupational safety regulations, dismissed him from his job. The official reason for his termination was that they let him go for his own protection and for being "physically unfit" to perform the work assigned to him. In addition to the embarrassment of losing his job, a highly prized opportunity that his father-in-law had arranged, Sam was facing the daunting task of trying to provide for a wife and four children without the security of a good-paying factory job. Suddenly out of work, he scrambled to find a job, any job at this point, since he had mouths to feed. He heard that they were hiring at the Cooper foundry and promptly applied. Although they brought him on, his stint there didn't last long. It isn't clear whether word about his potential health problems got around to other factory employers, but Cooper Bessemer let him go not too long afterwards. He never got hired on at any of the other industrial concerns, even those where several other local Black men had landed laborer positions. Those jobs, however, almost all involved working with the huge blast furnaces. The clear dangers at that factory were driven home when one of their number, Horace Rouse, was involved in a workplace accident and killed on the job.

Going door-to-door looking for work, Sam finally was hired to be a stock boy by a local five and dime department store, S. S. Kresge's. He worked hard to prove himself a dependable employee, eventually convincing his boss to increase his hours so he could do janitorial work after the store closed. Since the owners rented out the second floor of the building to other businesses and for professional offices, he was offered the job of cleaning all of the second-floor offices as well. All day, Sam climbed the steps that opened from the Gambier Street sidewalk down into the basement to stock or retrieve goods to be sold on the main floor of the store. In the evenings, he would climb the steep stairs that began at the alley to reach the offices on the second floor. Decades later, I wondered if he was ever permitted to ride the electric chair that was installed to help the disabled reach the doctor's office upstairs. Nearly fifty years after his passing, I was on that second floor among the offices where he had cleaned. My wife had her art studio there, and I swore to her that I felt an odd presence in that space. I couldn't say for sure that his spirit remained within that structure, but the hairs inexplicably rose on my neck when I walked the narrow hallway.

Despite his occasional bouts of dizziness, Sam refused to believe that something could be seriously wrong with him. He thought that he was just working too hard or becoming light-headed after getting up too quickly. Yet, the signs were there. This once athletic guy who would proudly prance on the high diving board at the Hiawatha Community Pool or strut around his yard without a shirt, was struggling to climb the stairs to do his work. It wasn't long before another spell occurred and then another. If he didn't do something soon, it may be just a matter of time before his body was found crumpled at the bottom of the stairwell. Oneida convinced him to go see the physician for whom his sister-in-law Ina Mae worked as a maid. The doctor had his suspicions that a neurological disorder was the cause and arranged for Sam to be examined at the VA Hospital in Cleveland where his veterans' benefits would pay for the treatment.

What began as something Sam thought would be a precautionary examination turned into years of frequent and sometimes long-term stays at the veterans' hospital. Eventually, the diagnosis was multiple sclerosis, a debilitating disease that would likely leave him permanently disabled. Some doctors thought that his affliction could have been related to his time in the military since he had served for a time in the Asiatic Pacific Theatre during World War II. It was later discovered that a significant number of soldiers who served in the Pacific during the war began to show signs of this and other diseases. Some of the white veterans were declared permanently disabled and received sizeable disability checks for the remainder of their lives. Not so for Sam. In between hospital stays, he did his best to find a job. It wasn't easy, since the nerve damage caused by the MS left him with symptoms of pain, fatigue, and loss of coordination. It was heartbreaking for Oneida when she saw him suddenly lose his balance and fall headlong to the ground. Yet, as his dad often reminded him, he had a family to support. Increasingly, he became racked with guilt that he wasn't doing more to provide for them. I didn't doubt that it would have been even worse for him if he had learned that white veterans who suffered the way that he did were approved for the kinds of benefits that would have allowed him to support his wife and kids and generally make his life better.

CHAPTER 10

A MAN'S PRIDE

If at one point Sam had ever thought that the Veterans Administration Hospital would be the answer to his problems, it soon became clear that it neither offered a cure for his afflictions nor did it ease his nagging thoughts that he might never again be normal. Though the VA doctors initially disagreed as to the precise diagnosis, there was little disagreement about his prognosis for recovery. It was bleak. Since they couldn't pinpoint the cause of the neurological disorder, they had no idea how to arrest the symptoms. More discouraging was their admission that the blackouts and spells that had stolen his job from him, and to a large degree his dignity, were likely to continue to occur, oftentimes without warning. The pain and frequent muscle spasms could leave him lying on the floor curled up in a fetal position. It was bad enough that his young wife had to witness his loss of control, but the thought that his children might find him so debilitated was almost unbearable. Like most sufferers of the disease, he found himself vacillating between periods of relapses and remissions. On one day, he might feel fully recovered and ready to take on the world; on the next, he sometimes wished that he could just die. And, so, it would go along like that for weeks, weeks that turned into months, and months that became years.

Sam was persistent in his efforts to find work. On the days that he was symptom free, he would set out to make the rounds of potential employers. He knew that many of the colored men in town, not fortunate enough to get on at a factory, held jobs as porters, janitors, bellmen, and general laborers. He had no reason to expect any better, and eventually he got work as a part-time janitor at the Episcopal Church. In addition, he occasionally got small jobs as a handyman for a family whose East Gambier Street house his mother-in-law cleaned. Sometimes he served as a driver for a well-to-do widower who lived in a grand house on North Main Street. He cleaned offices and did general painting jobs when he could get them. To help ease his disappointment at being limited to doing odd jobs, he called himself a self-employed contractor. During one period of remission in 1955, he even accepted a part in a local theatrical production presented during the sesquicentennial of the founding of Mt. Vernon. Of course, he joked, the role in which he was cast needed

News Photo
PLAYS BUTLER: Sam Sheffield plays the role of a butler in the reception scene at the H. B. Curtis home in the Sesquicentennial pageant.

FIGURE 10.1. The irony was not lost on Sam that he would be offered the role of a butler in the local theatrical production, a role he had come to know well in his life. Courtesy of *Mount Vernon News.*

no special study or preparation. He felt that after his recent work experiences, he was a natural. In the play, he portrayed a butler.

Pride can make men do desperate things and take drastic measures. No one knows for sure how much Sam's deteriorating physical condi-

tion took its toll on his personality. The once gregarious, outgoing fel-
low was becoming morose. The man who chastised friends and family
members for giving candy to one of his children but not the others was
becoming increasingly withdrawn. The man who once scolded his sister
when she warned that his children's wild antics with cans of whipped
cream would create an awful mess in his car would now barely respond
with his customary "It's their car, Lula; so, let them be." The days of
rough and tumble on the living room floor, one child pulling at each
leg and a third with her arms wrapped tightly around his neck, were
becoming part of what seemed like the distant past. It wasn't for lack of
desire, but his body wasn't responding to his pleas to straighten up and
act right. Sapped of strength and losing coordination, he barely recognized the man he saw in the mirror.

Self-esteem is crucial in a marriage. A man, especially of that
era, needed to feel good about himself and the contributions that he
brought to his relationship with his wife. It was important to him to
be secure in knowing that he was taking care of his family. Sam had
neither anymore, despite his constant efforts and regardless of how
important it was to him and them. As much as he wanted to control
his outbursts, they were happening with greater frequency . . . sometimes for what seemed like no reason at all. He complained about little
things, while she responded that it was hard trying to manage and keep
it all together alone. He knew that she meant not just when he was
at the VA hospital but even sometimes when he was living at home.
He struggled to act like the same ole Sam when he was around his
family. It was worse when his parents came to town on their way to
visit his sister Geneva, who was a resident of the state sanitarium in
Mt. Vernon. She, and later his older sister Lula, were diagnosed with
tuberculosis, a disease that removed patients from their families and
isolated them among others similarly ill. The closest TB hospital was
only a couple of miles from his home, and his parents regularly visited
on their way through. He didn't want them to see him in his debilitated state, failing to support his family as his father had reminded him
about over and over.

FIGURE 10.2. Visits by his father (R) were a mixed blessing for Sam Jr. (L), who so much wanted to meet his father's expectations as a good provider despite Sam Jr.'s increasing feeling that he was incapable of doing so.

By the winter of 1957, Sam and Oneida had four children under the age of nine and by that time had become accustomed to being financially strapped. Even though he worked less regularly, he continued to resist his young wife's offer to go out and get a job. He insisted that she was needed at home to take care of the children. Whether he didn't trust himself to be able to care for them alone or, once again, his pride couldn't handle having his wife become the breadwinner, he didn't want her to go to work. Regardless of his stubborn pride, they both worried about him having a spell in front of the children without

FIGURE 10.3. Their third child, Debra, displays the joy and excitement that Sam and Oneida's kids felt around the holidays in the Sheffield household.

another adult there to take over. She can't recall how they actually made it through that winter, but somehow the utilities got paid and they, with the help of her mother, managed to put food on the table. It helped going next door and stepping into the pantry or cellar to carry away enough to make dinner that evening. As the holidays approached, their finances didn't improve. If there would be presents that Christmas, they would have to be things that the kids needed instead of what they dreamed about or gleefully added to their lists for Santa. When they each opened the smartly wrapped boxes that cold December morning, there were four identical sets of tan, one-piece pajamas and matching caps with a puffy white ball at the end. After trying them on, the kids looked like four little elves decked out in onesies. The children's parents made sure that each of them had one other special item to unwrap, something inexpensive but intended to take into account their individual personalities and wishes. Although there was no money to create piles of presents, Oneida could always count on her mother and sisters to provide a few small items to make each child's haul appear to be much larger than it was. The main goal was to make sure that everyone had the same number of gifts, although Gregg, the oldest, made it his responsibility to count them and make note of the relative size of each box. There may have been one or two other gifts that Christmas, but none was as memorable for her as those "jammies."

CHAPTER 11

THE UNHAPPIEST OF
BIRTHDAYS

Winter, sometimes, has a way of lingering regardless of how anxious one is for spring to arrive. No matter the forecast, Oneida was looking forward to celebrating her birthday. It didn't even matter that on the second of March she would turn thirty, an age that her friends told her would finally mark her as a middle-aged woman. Her best friend, Sue, had invited her to come to Columbus to spend the night. Even though Oneida invited Sam to come along on her birthday trip, she knew that he would decline. To be perfectly honest, she wasn't disappointed that he did.

In declining to go along, Sam claimed that he had some important things that needed tending and couldn't wait. Besides, he said, she'd have a better time if he wasn't there. This way, he explained, she wouldn't be worrying the whole time if he was doing all right or have to leave earlier than she had planned because of him. While he believed those sentiments, he found himself saying them mostly to make her change her mind about going. It could have been that he just wanted to celebrate her birthday alone with her the way the two of them did before they had children. It might also have been a strong feeling that he needed her there to help him fend off the demons that had begun to haunt him.

FIGURE 11.1. As the weight of a troubled marriage bore down heavily, Oneida sought a break from the conflict in the company of her best friend, Sue Hairston.

Sam's words stung Oneida; she took them as him saying that she shouldn't be going out of town on her birthday. She received them as questioning her loyalty to him and the kids. It was as if he was saying that she shouldn't go because she had a family that wanted to be with her, too. Who did she think was more important anyway? She hated that he made her feel guilty just because she wanted . . . no, she needed, to have some fun and time for herself away from the stress and tension in the marriage. It wasn't fair that he made it into an act of betrayal. Of course, she loved her children . . . and him, but was she so wrong to want a break . . . just one day? And, no, she didn't plan to leave him without the car; Sue would come to pick her up. Damn, she had hoped to avoid an argument that would ruin her birthday. It wasn't even clear if there had been an argument or not, but once more she found herself feeling hurt. Sometimes he could make her feel guilty without ever raising his voice or using harsh language. It was just something in that tone and sullen look of his that left her feeling bad about herself regardless of the outcome.

Sue had planned to drive over to Mt. Vernon on Friday, February 28th and pick Oneida up to spend the night with her in Columbus; she'd bring her back Saturday afternoon. The birthday outing with Sue on Friday became a blur, however. Oneida was never able to fully remember much about it at all. The doctor said that a lot of her memories could have been erased by the shock of losing her husband. It was hard enough to accept that Sam was dead, but how he died wounded her deeply. Even the words spoken on the phone call placed to summon her home are buried deep somewhere that would never be retrieved. Yet, when her mother told her that his body had been found by the children, she was devastated. Just the thought of her two youngest coming into the living room, finding him dead in an infinite pool of blood wounded her like a knife to the heart. Just imagining the horror that Debra and Ricci must have felt when they walked into the house that morning left her crumpled in a heap on the floor. Would she . . . could she ever forgive herself?

There is no record nor is anyone living who may know when or how long it was before Deputy Sheriff Lousy arrived that Saturday. It's likely that the sheriff's office wasn't called until after Oneida returned. Sue, not sure how to be of help to her best friend, started almost immediately to clean up the blood, stopping only because she found the note. Written in the distinctive penmanship that Oneida had so admired from the day she first read a letter from Sam, the words were all a blur to her. Through the tears, she struggled to see and understand what had been said. The contents of the note, under circumstances like those, couldn't even begin to explain "why." Not able to comprehend what had happened . . . or even to think, she gave the note to Sue telling her that no one should ever see it. In the presence of Mary Jane, she pleaded for her best friend and sister to promise that her children would never see or learn about the note. As a good friend might do, Sue tucked it away in her purse.

When the sheriff's deputy and the coroner, Dr. James C. McLarnan, arrived and entered the front door, there lying on the living room floor was Sam's body, a bullet hole over the right eye. On a card table was gun-cleaning fluid and a rag, and on the floor beside his body was

a discharged .410 shotgun and a cleaning rod. Statements were taken
from the women huddled together in the house, attempting to comfort
Oneida as well as one another, including her mother, who had been
watching the children just a house away while her daughter was gone
for the evening in Columbus. The deputy ordered them not to touch
anything. As hard as it was to see, they were to leave things just as they
found them until the coroner had a chance to survey the scene. At least
he allowed them to go over to her mother's house to ask his questions.
Her sister took charge of the kids while the deputy sought answers.
Oneida couldn't recall what she was asked or what she said in response;
her mind went blank for a time. How long she couldn't say, but it was
probably only a few minutes that felt more like hours.

Oneida was asked many of the same questions, this time by the
coroner. Yes, Sam had experience handling a gun, having been in the
military and growing up hunting with his father. No, he had not been
hunting recently; she wasn't sure when the last time was, but it had
been quite a while. No, he didn't clean his gun very often; she couldn't
remember the last time that he did. No, she could not think of anyone
who would want to hurt Sam. Yes, he seemed upset when she last saw
him the day before, but he'd been frustrated about his health problems. No, she didn't think that he was angry enough to hurt himself.
Yes, they had had an argument . . . a small one. Yes, they were having some trouble in the marriage, but nothing any different than what
most couples experience from time to time. No, he wouldn't have . . .
he couldn't have . . . taken his own life. He wouldn't have done that to
the children . . . to her. Did he leave a note? She paused . . . and then
said she didn't know since everyone was trying to keep her away so she
didn't see his body.

It was ironic that the Mt. Vernon death announcements appeared
in the *News* adjacent to the local column announcing marriages and
births. There was nothing either celebratory or consoling in the stark
headline, "Coroner to Rule in Sheffield Death." Unlike the two other
death notices appearing that day, each reading like an ordinary obitu-
ary, the story about Sam's demise began like the opening of a crime
novel, "A ruling is expected today in the death of Samuel W. Sheffield,

Jr., 35, who was found dead in the living room of his home 12 Miami Street at 8:30 a.m. Saturday." Even for readers of that article who were neither family members nor close acquaintances of his, the details appearing in the article about his death were stunning. From the type of gun to the graphic images conjured up by a frank description of the distance the shotgun must have been from his head and the resulting damage inflicted, the article was so blunt that Oneida couldn't bring herself to read it. Sam's mother, Tillie, told the *Coshocton Tribune* just a couple days prior that she was informed by the coroner that her son died while cleaning his gun. But things just didn't add up. What experienced hunter would clean a loaded gun or not know that it was loaded? Why was he cleaning a gun that he hadn't used in years and didn't have plans to go hunting that anyone knew? The young man had serious health concerns and was struggling financially.

It was unusual, but the coroner, Dr. McLarnan, withheld his verdict for more than 48 hours after examining the body. He asked Oneida again, "Are you sure that he didn't leave a note?" Then, she told him that her friend had found a note, and to protect the kids took it with her back to Columbus. He immediately called Sue and told her that she had to bring the note back, that it was evidence in the case, and that he'd be waiting for her at the sheriff's office. As she arrived in Mt. Vernon, Sue stopped at Bertha's house to check on her friend before going to see the sheriff. For whatever reason, Oneida told her that she wanted to read the note one last time. Then she pulled out a pen and paper and began to copy down the words, slowly between her sobs, staring at the page, weirdly caught between being a grieving widow and a painstaking stenographer. After carefully copying and transferring the words to her own page, she folded it in half, opened her Bible, and gently placed the paper inside. Her friend then delivered the note to the sheriff.

Shortly after receipt of the note on Monday, March 3rd, the coroner issued his findings that Sam's death was the result of suicide and released them to the press. In Tuesday's *Mt. Vernon News*, the headline declared, "Sheffield Death Ruled Suicide." As if meant to support the coroner's conclusion, the article restated the details including where the shot pierced his head after being fired "within six inches of the eye." Sam's parents felt that the story was cruel and insensitive to give such detail of the killing, but what broke Oneida's heart was the report that he "had made threats recently against his wife, Oneida, who was in Columbus at the time Sheffield was killed. Dr. McLarnan said Mrs. Sheffield had not separated from her husband, but was only in Columbus temporarily." To have the details of their marriage opened to the public was upsetting, but she took some relief that at least the existence of the note was not disclosed as well. Over the decades, the note continued to haunt her, and she tried on several occasions to build up her strength to destroy it altogether. When she finally went to retrieve it many years later, she couldn't help but notice that it was pressed firmly between the pages, one of which contained Nehemiah 8:10. She read it softly aloud to herself, "Do not grieve, for the joy of the Lord is your strength." And she took comfort in knowing that His hand guided her to that moment and beyond. I was never able to convince her to show me the note. Apparently, she shredded it as she had planned, or maybe she had tucked it away somewhere long since forgotten, perhaps never to surface again.

For many years, decades in fact, Oneida could not bring herself to talk about her husband's death. She insisted on telling her children that their father was killed in a hunting accident, repeating the narrative that Tillie Mae had created, and begged her mother and sisters to never tell them any different. Fiercely protective of them, she committed herself to filling them with wonderful, positive stories about Sam and his unwavering devotion to them. While the older ones had a better sense that things they knew and were hearing from her, and others as well, didn't quite jibe, they took comfort in her stories and allowed the younger ones to believe as much as they could.

It was strange growing up with few people ever mentioning my father, almost as if he didn't exist. Perhaps, they thought that by talking about him they would run the risk of revealing this closely guarded family secret that was really only a secret to us, his children. But just because they didn't bring him up didn't mean that others in the neighborhood, our teachers and schoolmates, and nearly everyone else we had contact with didn't know that we were the poor children whose father had killed himself. It wasn't until many years later that she learned that her sister, Mary Jane, had betrayed her trust and told Oneida's older daughter about the letter. She hadn't thought far enough ahead to realize that as the children got older that their need for answers and closure would lead them to ask the questions that for years were never discussed in her household. Nearly fifty years later, she seemed somewhat relieved to no longer have to guard her secret. While still very difficult to discuss, she admitted that she never had or took the time to come to terms with my father's death. Maybe, just maybe, our conversation that day started her on the path toward healing.

CHAPTER 12

I'D SWEEP THE STREETS
IF I HAD TO

Life for a young widow with four small children was more than difficult. There was no time to wallow in her own grief nor time to even begin to process it. Oneida needed to ensure that her family was provided for. More importantly, she needed to make sure that they all stayed together. Shortly after Sam's death, Tillie Mae told Oneida that she, of all people, understood well how hard things could be for a widowed mother to care for her large family. She could speak from her own experience having lost her first husband while raising five children. With no life insurance benefits and no job, how could Oneida think that she could possibly make do? Of course, as her mother-in-law pointedly reminded, her kids were too young for her to work outside the home, so there were no prospects for her financial situation to improve. So, Tillie tried to convince her that it might be best if the children went to live with some members of her family.

Sam's brother Claude Robert and his wife, Arsenia, were childless. They had suffered through her miscarriages and had not been blessed with a child of their own. Oneida's mother-in-law told her that they might be willing to take two of the children. Tillie thought that she might be able to talk Sam's other younger brother, Maurice, and his wife into doing the same. Oneida was horrified by the thought that they would even suggest or might try to take her children from her.

FIGURE 12.1. It was important to Oneida that her children always feel loved and supported. Living with her mother helped her do that.

For at least a moment, her anger exceeded her fear, and she said some things to her mother-in-law that are perhaps best never repeated. She made it clear to everyone that she would do anything and everything in her power to make sure that her children stayed together and with her. On more than one occasion, she declared that if necessary she would take a broom and sweep the streets if that's what it took to keep everyone together. With God's help, it would work. Even without it, she would never give them up.

Oneida and her four children moved in with her mother, Bertha. Since I was not quite four years old and my Grandma Hammonds lived only two houses away, it didn't seem at the time like such a monumental change for me. Fairly soon thereafter, my mother managed to rent out our house to a colored family in town; the Crossons were friends and in need of a place that spring. She, of course, badly needed the rental income, and it was a reasonably comfortable arrangement for the time being. She quickly landed a job as a nurse's aide, a "candy-striper" they were called because of the white uniform with the red stripes running down its length that vaguely resembled a candy-cane. This type of job had been filled mostly by volunteers, but a sympathetic administrator at the aptly named Mercy Hospital took pity and offered her a paid position. Working the "graveyard shift" from 11 p.m. until 7 a.m., Oneida left her children each evening in the charge of her mother, heading out after they had gone to bed and returning each morning before they got up. Other than her suffering through constant sleep deprivation over the ensuing months, she was able to maintain a relatively normal schedule for her kids. She was there when they started the day, sitting around the dining room table in their pajamas chatting over bowls of Rice Krispies along with half a piece of toast. The toast was always cut on a diagonal and slightly burnt since Grandma Hammonds didn't want anyone to touch the toaster settings after she had gotten it exactly where she liked it best.

Once Oneida got her children up, dressed, and outside to play, she would try to get some greatly needed sleep. The kids eventually learned after several reminders that we were expected to play in the backyard away from the front bedroom where we were told that our mother was taking a nap and didn't want to be disturbed. My grandmother found a variety of ways to keep us occupied as well as get her chores done. I couldn't count how often I spent time picking seeds from her ornamentals and collecting black poppy seeds in a tin can. One day, we would pinch the flowering four o'clocks until the seeds exploded out of the top; the next day we'd trim the rose bush that climbed the lattice trellis beside the chicken coop-turned-playhouse. Most afternoons, we cut fresh bouquets of orangish-yellow marigolds or whatever else was in bloom to put on the supper table for our mother. She never failed to make a fuss about our thoughtfulness.

Each of the children had their own chores to do around my grandmother's house. Adhering to traditional gender norms, the boys' assignments involved yard work and household maintenance, even though we didn't know much at all about fixing stuff. We were doing well to know where our grandmother kept her toolbox and the difference between a hammer and a wrench. Our ability to actually use the tools was something altogether different. Our main job was to mow the lawn. Initially, we used Poppy's old manual mower with the dullest blades imaginable. It tended to push the blades of grass down rather than cut them. Later, when our grandmother purchased a power mower, I would try to mow as quickly as I could, oftentimes running behind it to get this chore over with as soon as possible.

The girls were expected to follow in the footsteps of all of the women in the family. Debi learned to dust and run the old Hoover vacuum cleaner with the over-filled cloth bag that spewed out more dirt than it actually picked up. When special occasions came around, she would help polish the silverware and set the table with the good china that spent most of each year carefully put away in the black, wooden China cabinet. "Them deeshes," as my Aunt Mary reminded us, were very valuable and had to be handled with extra care. I would sometimes stare at them through the cabinet glass wondering what made them any nicer than the plastic colored plates on which we usually ate our meals.

Karen was taught to fill the old wringer washing machine that was positioned like a sentry on the south side of the back porch. That porch proved to be cursed for her since it was also the site of my brother's mistaken belief that getting shot in the eye by a pop gun loaded with salt was less painful than one loaded with pepper. His curiosity resulted in my sister nearly losing sight in her left eye. But that was the lesser of traumas for her on that porch. While learning to guide the wet clothes from the agitating tub through the wringer, her tiny fingers got stuck between the rollers. By the time my grandmother was able to shut the wringer down, my sister's arm had been pulled through the tight rollers clear up to the elbow. After my grandmother slammed the machine into reverse, continuing to squeeze her limp arm like a metal

HIAWATHA
1958-59

FIGURE 12.2. Karen Sheffield was well liked by her elementary school teachers and classmates.

press, the damage had been done. Karen suffered broken bones in that arm and had to wear a cast for several weeks. I can't recall if she was expected to do any chores the rest of that year. She spent her days trying to wear her cast so that it didn't clash with any of the outfits that she had picked out to wear to school.

By the spring of 1959, Oneida was receiving modest social security benefits that were available for surviving spouses and children of men who had passed. While it wasn't much, it was just enough to allow her to return to her house with her kids. Her best friend, Sue, encouraged her to apply for public assistance, but my mother didn't want people to think that she was lazy or unable and unwilling to take care of her family on her own. Whether it was her pride or the lack of understanding about what help was available to deserving families, she tried to make do without it. Still, it was important to her that she and her children get back into their house before the next school year. Everything was geared toward trying to achieve some sense of normalcy for her children. Although, it was difficult to imagine how anything could ever be normal again after the loss of her husband and the father of her children to an act of suicide, even when the word *suicide* was never to be mentioned around her kids.

That fall, the three older children were back in school. It was just she and her youngest, Ricci, together during the days. To earn some additional money to help make ends meet, Oneida began to take in laundry like many of the older colored women in our town had always done. She wasn't fond of doing it, but it meant a few extra dollars. She couldn't help but be reminded of the stories her mother would tell her of having to make her own lye soap to do the washing. "Four pounds of grease; one can of lye," and before you knew it the Borax and water would bring that pungent smell of soap to life. She didn't care much for washing clothes, but ironing didn't bother her at all. In fact, she always said that ironing was a time when she could retreat into her own thoughts and escape from the things that brought her worry and stress. She'd drop down the ironing board that was hidden away in a cupboard that Sam had rigged up in the tiny hallway of their house, a constant reminder that there was so little room. Every inch of space was carefully utilized; even so, there was never enough room to have a washing machine, assuming she had managed to find a way to pay for one. Besides, the meager water pressure from the underground well that fed our pipes probably would have taken most of the day to complete a couple of loads of wash.

For most of my youth, we made weekly trips to Ringold Street Laundry Mat with clothes baskets stacked high in the back seat of the car, almost blocking her view to the window behind. In the summers, she'd hang the wet clothes on the clothesline, oftentimes filling up our line and having to spill over onto Aunt Inee's line next door. In the winter, she'd stuff as many clothes as she could into the 25-cent dryers to get them "mostly dry." She had discovered that a hot iron could finish them up while saving her a few coins. She'd always start with the baskets that the white ladies would bring by, while her own laundry would have to wait dampened and rolled up in the refrigerator until it was their turn. She could stand there at the ironing board for hours, earning the paltry sum of ten cents a shirt, sprinkling and pressing . . . spraying and starching, one shirt after another. To keep her five-year-old from being underfoot while she worked, she set up a tiny ironing board with a miniature iron. She'd tell me what a great help it was to her to have me laboring over the creases of the handkerchiefs for which she was paid a penny apiece. It didn't seem to matter to her that she had to redo each hankie that I attempted. I never caught on that the iron wouldn't work without being plugged in which she was sure not to allow lest I burned myself.

Within another year, all four of Oneida's children were attending Hiawatha School, less than four blocks from their home. At the time,

I gave it no mind that it was the only school in the area named after native peoples or any persons of color, but I later saw the irony that the only brown-skinned woman ever to serve as an officer of the school's Parents Teachers Association was a descendant of an Indian great-grandmother and was named after a well-known tribe. My mother took her involvement in her children's education very seriously and remembered how important her own schooling was to her own mother. Even before then, she would make her way to meetings at her niece Betty Lou's school since her sister, Mary Jane, never seemed to have time or the inclination to show up to support her own daughter. Maybe that was one of the reasons that my mother was so adamant about supporting her own children's schooling. Many a night, the five of us sat around the blond-wood dinner table doing homework together, she moving from child to child to help us solve arithmetic problems, practice our spelling, or learn to pronounce new vocabulary words.

On one occasion in particular, she didn't hesitate one bit to march right down to the elementary school to confront the principal, Howard Wacker, when an insensitive fifth-grade teacher, Evelyn Genre, thought nothing of her customary practice of reading aloud *Huck Finn* and *Tom Sawyer* to her class. And there sat my brother, Gregg, as this genteel Georgia native leisurely strolled through the passages that seem to use the word *nigger* time and time again. My mother told me how it made her blood boil, and how much she appreciated the support that she received from Mr. Wacker. The principal emphatically told Mrs. Genre that she may not assign books in which "that word" appeared and that she should never have read it aloud to the children in the first place.

As one might expect, Principal Wacker's edict was too little and too late. And, it certainly wasn't as though that word materialized for the first time in our lives during a school reading period. My initial memory of hearing that word took place while I was walking home from school in first grade with older children calling it out repeatedly behind me. The substance and context of their words didn't stay with me, but the meanness of their intent was unmistakable. I guess that was the first indication that I would later, and for much of my life, take

FIGURE 12.3. Debra Sheffield, from an early age, was the most
independent and outspoken of Oneida's children.

on a stoic veneer seeming to be impervious to threats and offense. I
didn't show that it affected me then, just as I rarely had shown that it
affected me on the many other occasions throughout my life when I
felt I was being singled out because of my race. Those daily short walks
home for lunch took on new meaning. It was not the customary lun-
cheon fare of fried baloney sandwiches and dill pickles that left a bad
taste in my mouth on those days when my lunches were preceded by
such taunts. Despite my efforts to hide that something was wrong, my
mother could always tell. With a comforting smile, she'd tell me that
she was planning a special dinner that evening just for me. To tide me
over, she'd reach into the cabinet over the breadbox and pull out one
of those sticky sweet Hostess treats that kids clamor for so often. Even
though she'd tell us that they weren't good for growing kids, somehow, she managed to find my favorite, the chocolate cupcakes with the
cream filling, perhaps put away for just such an occasion. I suspect that
she did the same for Gregg, who was partial to Sno Balls laced with
vanilla-coconut icing, or the soft spongy Twinkies that my sisters preferred when they had their run-ins with some of the school kids who

made it their habit to tease children who were different from them. On occasions like those, she would dip deeply into her well of encouraging sayings that I'm sure came from Lon Hammonds. "When you cross the room, hold your head up high and keep moving forward just like you own it."

For a relatively tiny building, Hiawatha School seemed enormous to me when I started there. From the playground to the long lines of children moving in and out of the massive double doors for recess, I had never before been in the company of dozens of children of different sizes and ages in a single place. Despite their discernible differences in one respect as all of the grades comingled on the playground, they were also all alike in another. All of the more than one hundred children spread out over six grades and classrooms were white. Except that is, for the school's seven Black kids, four of whom lived in my household and a fifth, my cousin Bill, who lived next door. The other two, Linda and Donny Glover, lived with their grandparents and walked the six blocks to our neighborhood school. The Glovers had come to live with their father's parents in order to attend what their parents believed was a better school than the one that they had been attending in Columbus. Their father, a native of Mt. Vernon, was not only concerned about the quality of their education but for their safety. He had seen firsthand how children in the city easily got involved in activities that led to trouble or worse. He feared that his children would experience the same if they remained in the big city's public schools.

My second-grade teacher, Mrs. Demorest, was a pleasant enough younger teacher who seemed to have a genuine fondness for me. I liked that she was new since it was hard sometimes to attend a school in which you followed after three older siblings. Teachers would often remark how much you were either alike or different from your brother or sisters. While that could be good when the characteristics they associate with you were generally positive, it could also put a lot of pressure on you, stunting your ability to get out from under them to establish yourself. We all wanted to be our own person. I quickly learned, however, that a lot was expected of me early on. Because my siblings had generally done well in school, I was supposed to do well. Since my brother and sisters had been mannerly and well behaved, there was every expectation that I would be the same. And, of course, I didn't disappoint. I couldn't have been any more compliant. Even though my classmates and friends were occasionally on the business end of the menacing paddle that hung ominously by the door to the classroom, I went through all six years of grade school without ever facing any discipline. My ambition was simply to be liked by my teachers and classmates . . . and, of course, to get to be on the school crossing-guard patrol as my siblings had done and that I thought was the coolest thing in the world. But, I never had the opportunity to do it when Hiawatha School was converted into a junior high school just as I was about to enter the sixth grade and become eligible to wear the white belt and silver badge that marked the trusted students assigned to the patrol.

CHAPTER 13

MANAGING TO GET BY

There's much about those early years after our father's death that wasn't known to any of Oneida's children. How she managed to carry on both physically and emotionally is a mystery. If things were tough financially before Sam's death, they didn't get a whole lot better for years afterwards. Many folks often say that they didn't realize it at the time that they had grown up poor. I suppose the same can be said for our family, but doing without things seemed so much less important than doing without a husband and a father. Since we had a roof over our heads, the utilities got paid, eventually, and her kids didn't go to bed hungry, there wasn't any discussion of hardships. She was quick to remind us that there were millions of people in the world much worse off than we were. And we believed her. From time to time, she'd recite what her grandfather used to say when things got tough: "If you wait for the world to be perfect, you'll be waiting a long time. Before you know it, you will have forgotten just what it was that you had been waiting for."

Oneida didn't just remind her children how fortunate they were, she often showed them how proud she was that they were doing "ok . . . just fine, thank you," in the same manner that she replied when asked by friends and neighbors how things were going. When visitors came to our home for the first time, she often offered to give them a tour of our tiny house. I didn't realize it at the time, but it wasn't because there was anything special about our modest home to show off. To the contrary, it was in many ways fairly ordinary and nondescript, even a bit on the small, cramped side. I believe that what she wanted people to see more than anything was how clean and well-maintained she kept our house. While there was nothing particularly impressive about the smallish structure, I think that her offering to show it to those visiting our home for the first time was her way of saying, "Look what I've been able to do," and against all odds. She took enormous pride in that, and I'm sure that was something she learned from her mother. I realize now where I got that from. I also have a much greater appreciation for the satisfied smile that crept across her face on those occasions when she'd throw back her head and proclaim, "Lord knows, we got by."

My childhood memories are filled with recollections of sitting at the picnic table in Bertha's backyard snapping green beans until my fingers were worn down to nubs. I'd toss the remnants into my grandmother's giant metal pot with a round wooden grip on the steel handle that reminded me of a large spindle for thread. Snap—toss, snap—toss, again and again as the green mound rose. And just when I thought we had finished, she would refill the basket from the brown paper bag that I had dragged from plant to plant in the garden. Conversations among those at the table always led to reminiscing about the days down on the farm. Whenever I would tire of snapping beans and begin to fuss about how worn out I was, Aunt Mary would be the one to remind all of us at the table about the humble beginnings from which our family came. "Boy," she said, "we were so poor that we barely had a pot to piss in, let alone a window to throw it out of. Then it'd be just our luck that the wind was blowin' back in our direction." She'd always say it in the same way and look deep into your face to make sure you got the point. She finished her thought with, "So, you better feel grateful to have shoes to wear and a shirt on your back. We didn't have that when we were growing up."

Food bills overall for our houses and the rest of the entire extended family were generally lower because of the community harvests and preparation that were done right there in my grandmother's yard. I was the one most often asked to climb up into her apple trees to shake the branches. Watching the ripest ones fall to the ground as I pushed against the tree was just a reminder of her promise to bake some fresh pies after she finished making the applesauce. She had a way of enticing me with visions of sweet delights, grape juice if I picked the grapes and delicious jam after I brought her a couple quarts of strawberries. I was often called upon to fetch items for her from the garden, and usually found myself pulling carrots and green onions from the rich black soil, rubbing them against my pant legs and biting down hard. Nothing compared, though, to the sun-ripened tomatoes as I anxiously wiped the dirt off with my t-shirt and bit down until the juice squirted out and raced down my chin. Nearly every bit of the produce in her gardens ended up in neatly stacked Mason jars that filled her pantry shelves. I have often thought over the years that I've not had a single vegetable in sixty years that tasted as fresh and delicious as what we enjoyed in those days.

CHAPTER 14

WANTING A CAREFREE LIFE
FOR THEM

It would not have been an exaggeration to characterize the childhood of each of Oneida's children as relatively carefree, even after the tragedy we experienced and the precariousness of our mother's financial situation. She was determined that we not feel as though we were somehow less than the neighborhood children because we had or could afford so much less than children in other families. So, she worked hard to manage what little money she earned to make sure that she could stretch every dime as far as it could possibly go.

When Oneida had to make choices as to which bills to pay and which to ask for more time, we were generally unaware. More than once when Mr. Richardson came to collect the insurance payment, he had to settle for 15 cents that week instead of the promised quarter.

Being financially strapped was a factor in the types of recreation that our family could afford. When in the summers we headed to the community swimming pool where we had a family pass, we weren't told we were lucky that someone had donated the funds that paid for "disadvantaged families" like ours to be able to swim as we were doing. When we visited the local YMCA, no one informed us that it was the former mayor of our town, Mr. Mauger, who had given the money for our family membership. On occasion, there were times when we discovered or were reminded that we were the recipients of some sort of charity, like that time that my sister's classmates teased her about wearing their old hand-me-downs that had been obtained from the local Goodwill store. I'll never forget my excitement to get what, for me, looked like an authentic football jersey that my Aunt Ina brought home from her job as a maid. Her employer's son, Doug, the shirt's former owner, was ready to throw it away, and she rescued it for me to wear. But I also remember that day in the school hallway as I proudly wore that blue jersey with the yellow lightning bolts splayed across each shoulder that he reminded me that it was only because he had tired of it that it was now mine. He wanted me to know that it wasn't nearly as cool as the new one that he got to replace it.

In farming and rural communities, it was not uncommon for children to trace the steps of their parents in many areas of life. Not only did Oneida's children attend the same elementary school that their mother did, they frolicked in the same yards and fields and along the same creek that were her play spaces. I suspect that in many ways our playtime was as much like hers as her playtime was like her mother's. As a child growing up on Miami Street, it felt at times like having one's own amusement park. When she was a child and Lon decided to reduce the number of chickens that he wanted to raise, they were consolidated in the larger coop. That meant that the smaller brooder house situated in a prominent place in the yard became my mother's playhouse. As a child, she loved that miniature house with a front door that couldn't have been more than four feet high so that grownups would have to bend over to come inside. The front featured a row of framed windows and a cupola on top. Lon made her a tiny table and a couple of chairs to keep in the playhouse to entertain her "guests," both make-believe and real. There is no way that she could have imagined that one day she would stand in front of her former playhouse and exchange marriage vows with the man she loved. It was probably more predictable for her to imagine that the former chicken coop would one day serve as a playhouse for her own children and most of the nieces and nephews in the family.

Eventually, raising chickens became too much for my grandparents, although my Uncle Stan kept it up in their coop for a while longer. But

Lon's days of keeping animals were gone, and it wasn't long before he was as well. He died when I was only a year old. So, my memories of the larger chicken coop were mostly as an old shed in a constant state of disrepair. Later, I would climb the tree that hung over the back to line up black walnuts on the corrugated tin roof so they would ripen. Grandma would give me a bucket and have me pick them up after they fell to keep the worms from burrowing inside. After a few days on the roof, their green skins would darken and dry so that they could be more easily opened, the shells cracked, and the nutty flesh taken out. I found out the hard way that the tin can lids that I'd grab up to expedite the shelling could slice clean through the stubborn outer skins if one wasn't careful. But two things like being careful and kids handling sharp tin can lids are opposites; they don't really go together. So, I managed to slice my finger or a thumb more times that I care to remember. That was almost as annoying as the handful of times that Uncle Stan gave me the job of feeding his chickens in that shed. Truth be told, I was afraid of them and would usually toss the entire pan of corn onto the ground and get out of the pen as quickly as I could. I didn't care that the more aggressive chickens would keep the others from eating. I couldn't have been happier when my uncle eventually decided that the occasional egg that he got wasn't worth the trouble. He got no argument from me. While the chickens were cheap, the rooster wasn't. And that old rooster had to be the most menacing creature on the farm. So, it wasn't long before my uncle gave up on that hobby.

Within a short time, the old chicken coop became the designated doghouse. I didn't like it any better and still had a fear of entering that space, even after our dog Ginger had her litter of puppies in there. My brother had convinced me that the outbuilding was home to a nest of lethal spiders that he said were to be found nowhere else in this world but in that shed. Unlike the typical fear of venomous insects, the concern wasn't that these long, stick-like creatures might bite us. We worried about how quickly they could count. Yes, spiders that counted. Every time we went to care for the dogs, he warned me that if the spiders counted my teeth that I would die. So, when I entered the shed to feed the dog or to fill her water bowl, I made sure to always cover my mouth and sometimes clamped down so hard that I would accidentally bite my lip. Of course, just as we got inside he made a habit of trying to make me laugh or make me cry out in fear just so my teeth were exposed and, I assumed, more easily countable. After my mother remarried, my stepfather built a big new doghouse at the edge of our backyard. So, my remaining years caring for the family canine were spent filling the water bowl and feeding Duke, a large mixed-breed dog that was strong enough to pull the rather large doghouse to which he was chained all the way up to the middle of our backyard. Believe me, the garbage collectors were not fans of that big dog. And we never worried about someone sneaking up to the back of our house.

Duke wasn't the largest animal that we had when we were kids. It must be obligatory for kids who live "out-in-the-country" (which is what our friends and the children of my parents' friends who lived in the city called it) to want to have a horse or pony at some point. I suppose I was no different, especially having grown up riding ponies several times a week throughout the summers. Our backyard was separated from a thirty-acre pony farm by a low, easily climbable barbed-wire fence under or through which we routinely slipped with only an occasional puncture wound on one of our hands or jagged scratch across the back. To the immediate south of our pony farm was a horse farm with an electric fence to keep the horses back from the standard fencing. It was just the type of barrier that tempted us time and time again to see if our reflexes were faster than the milliseconds it took the current to run up our fingers and arms to our brains, forcing us to let out a squeal. Looking back, I wondered whether brain damage might have occurred since we never quite learned that we couldn't touch and release the wire before getting shocked, nor did it occur to me that using a long blade of grass to touch the wire would not insulate me from hearing that crinkly zap at my fingertips.

Riding ponies along the well-worn paths on the perimeter of the farm was a common summer ritual, interrupted only by the forays down to the creek to ford the stream. The ponies knew the drill, sensing that the sooner they crossed, the quicker they could return to the barn and the tasty bales of hay. Except on those especially hot summer days when steam rose up from their backsides and the saddles became particularly oppressive, they were quite compliant. On the sweltering days, though, they would walk into the middle of the stream and pause as if to contemplate whether the cool waters cascading against their legs promised a greater relief than the shade trees that lined the route. Invariably my pony's head went down for a cool drink. I'd clutch as hard with my thighs as I could to keep from sliding off. The hottest days seemed to coax Lady, my usual mount, to engage in her unnerving habit of attempting to lie down in the shallow rapids. Strangely, I was more upset about the prospect of getting soppin' wet than the thought that this large animal could land on me and crush me with its weight.

Why it wasn't enough to climb the fence when we had daily access to the farm, I'll never know. Somehow, my sister persuaded our mother that having a pony of our own was the next best thing. After all, our next-door neighbors, the Browns, got a pony for their daughter, Kimmie. It only made sense that their pony, Jack, should have a companion. After our Uncle Stan, a man who hated for someone to have something that he didn't have, got his own pony, a Chincoteague Paint named Pumpkin, he agreed to help us acquire one of our own. The new pony was ostensibly for my sister, Deb, who begged our mother the most. Within a couple of weeks, there we were converting one of Poppy's old sheds in Aunt Ina's backyard adjacent to ours into a stall and loading it with straw and hay.

Jill, our new equine acquisition with a name fitting to be a companion for our neighbor's pony, Jack, spent most of her days at the end of a heavy chain staked into the ground, eating the grass down to the nub. That worked pretty well since Uncle John wasn't up to mowing anymore in addition to the fact that his rickety riding mower would rarely start. Despite her promises to be responsible for all the daily maintenance, my sister began almost immediately to negotiate with me to share these chores. In exchange for my help, she would say, it would be "our" pony. But it didn't take many days of cleaning out the stall before her enthusiasm for the work, if not the pony, waned. Her official excuse, at least the one that earned her the most sympathy from my mother, was her intense fear of snakes, creatures that seemed to be frequent residents among the hay bales in the horse shed. Whether she actually saw one or simply that her vivid imagination convinced her that snakes somehow always managed to be there on her day to shovel the manure into the large rubber bucket, it soon became clear that I was the only one regularly going into the shed to clean the stall and stack the heavy bales.

Debi tried to justify her reduced workload by the fact that she occasionally mowed lawns to earn a dollar to buy oats to feed the pony. Of course, at her young age someone had to take her into town to the Farmer's Exchange to purchase the oats. Those trips usually ended with her getting a delicious cold treat from the neighborhood Milk House dairy. And, it was my brother, Gregg, who bought a bridle for Jill, using money from his grocery-bagging job at the local IGA. Not that he wasn't ordinarily a generous person, but Gregg's real motivation was to be the first one to ride this pony that had only been partially broken. He took it as a challenge and wasn't deterred one bit when it kicked his friend Jack Welker square in the chest when they tried to insert a bit into her mouth.

Even as I began to fret about the prospect of the many pony chores when cold weather came, imagining myself slogging through deep snow to bring fresh water and stacking bales to block the wind that blew through the cracks in the walls of the shed, it became apparent that we weren't equipped or mature enough to adequately care for Jill through the winter season. My worries were for naught because by early fall, the pony was gone. The grownups decided for us that our plan to keep Jill in the unheated, dilapidated shed tended to by two less than enthusiastic stable hands was sure to fail. Over the most strenuous objection that Deb could muster given the circumstances, the pony was led down the road to the place from which she came. I liked to think that she was reunited with her family back at the farm, but I never was sure.

CHAPTER 15

ADVENTURE IN THE BLOOD

As children, I'm convinced that we had horseback- and pony-riding in our blood. It just happened to be from another source and on the other side of our family. My father's youngest brother was the closest thing to a horse whisperer that our family had. Uncle Maurice, an adventurer from his earliest days, had a special fondness for horses. As a boy, he managed to get odd jobs helping out on neighbors' farms, keeping his eyes peeled for any chance to work with horses. Already pretty much fearless, it was through those summer and after-school jobs that he learned to ride. And, man, did he learn to ride. Within a fairly short time, he was spending all of his spare time riding horses. He eventually developed a special affection for the rodeo, excited by the trick riders and the rough and tumble cockiness of a bucking bronco.

My educational experience in predominantly white and rural Mt. Vernon had not exposed me to anything approaching African American history, so I wasn't aware of the legendary Black cowboy Bill Picket or that there had been a Black cavalry unit known as the Buffalo Soldiers. I'm sure that I couldn't have imagined back then that men who looked like us—Myrtis Dightman and Charles Sampson—would one day be inducted into the Pro Rodeo Hall of Fame. Yet, I was enthralled by the stories that Uncle Maurice, the self-proclaimed "Clark Dark, Flying Cowboy from Africa," the name that appeared on his flashy business

To: Maurice,
The foreman of the Bar M Ranch!
Jim McClure

FIGURE 15.1. As if born to be a cowboy, Maurice Sheffield
was a natural when it came to riding horses.

card, would tell about his participation in a number of local rodeo competitions. He regaled us with his vivid descriptions of standing on the
backs of galloping horses that he claimed were in full stride or execut-
ing hand stands on the side of his mount. He took special pride in scor-
ing points for being able to stay on a menacing brahma bull for the full
eight-second count, but he wasn't nearly as anxious any more to try his
hand at "rasslin'" steers to the ground after they exploded out of the chute.
He tried, unsuccessfully, to show me how to tie a slipknot in a rope and
reminded me on more than one occasion not to sneak up on a horse from

FIGURE 15.2. Cowboy Maurice Sheffield believed that he was
meant to ride in every parade and lead the equestrian brigades.

behind. A frightened horse's kick, he assured me, could knock my head
"clean off." He never missed the opportunity to saddle up to join the
mounted entries in the local parades. As he drew near the corner where
our family was assembled on the sidewalk, he would make his horse
skip and dance as if to announce to an audience filled with white faces
that he had brought some color to the occasion.

I tended to believe anything that Uncle Maurice told me. Whether
he was apt to exaggerate just a bit or not, his was by far the most exciting life of anyone I knew. Wide-eyed and breathless, I was thrilled by

his stories of danger and daring. I shivered uncontrollably when he talked about burning the tires on his army truck to keep from freezing to death after it broke down one night during a tour of duty in Korea. I was glued to the tattered screen when he showed us home movies that he had taken while serving as a helicopter pilot in Viet Nam. At one such showing, I found myself instinctively leaning over as if my movements those many months later might have helped him guide his "bird" safely down to the deck of the ship upon which he was to land. Who could forget the rides in his custom-made dune buggy? If you looked up the definition of *adventurer* in the dictionary, it likely would have included a reference to Maurice Sheffield.

So, when Uncle Maurice arrived at our house one summer boasting of a special surprise, I thought my mother would faint after he announced that he was taking his nephews up for a ride in the four-seater Piper Cub that he had borrowed from a friend for the afternoon. He pulled up to our house driving his tiny German car that many thought looked like some kind of giant insect. Of course, he'd be one of the first to own a Volkswagen Beetle. I don't recall many of the details of the flight since my eyes were clenched tightly closed during both the takeoff and landing while it felt as though my stomach was slowly inching its way up to my throat. But, I'll never forget the wonder of seeing our postage stamp-sized house below and the rest of the family standing in the yard waving as the plane circled a couple of times directly overhead. Prior to that day, I had only dreamed of going up in an airplane and spent countless hours in my younger years trying to build one in my yard with leftover lumber and a rusted lawnmower engine that I found in my grandmother's garage. I'm sure that it probably had not been started for several years, but I was undeterred by my lack of knowledge about flying nor the fact that I had repeatedly failed to assemble an airworthy craft. So, my fantasies about one day flying high above had finally come to fruition through the efforts of a flying Black cowboy, the only pilot that I ever knew who looked like me.

CHAPTER 16

JUST A COUPLE OF BOYS
ON SAFARI

Except for that flight with Uncle Maurice, my adventures were limited to the much tamer forays on the ground just beyond my backyard. Each trip into the pony field behind our house was like going on safari. My job as the tagalong little brother was to remain quiet while Gregg slowly crept through the high grass and weeds hoping to come upon some unsuspecting prey. I usually carried a long stick that I wielded like a machete or found a staff, carefully carving a sharp point to make a spear, if I remembered to bring along a penknife. But, Gregg was the "bwana" on these excursions, although none of them on Johnny Weissmuller's popular Tarzan series were Black like us. From an early age, he had taken to archery. Starting with a toy bow and moving to a youth archery set, Gregg practiced often by shooting at tree trunks, logs, and other large inanimate objects. Later, he graduated to a twenty-pound recurve bow, prompted by the assurances of Ricky Poland, a neighbor boy whose father was one of those serious hunters and outdoorsmen that hung squirrel tails to the side of his garage. Now, with a real bow, my brother was certain that he would finally hit the small game that seemed to tease him as they scampered out of range. On more than one occasion, he claimed we'd be eating quail for dinner, although neither of us had ever had quail or knew that for some it was considered a delicacy. Looking back, I couldn't think of another single Black person

FIGURE 16.1. Gregg Sheffield (L) and his tagalong little brother, Ricci (R), who spent most days hard at play, take a break.

who hunted with a bow, especially one who actually was pretty skilled as an archer.

Almost daily, we'd venture down to the "crick" (which I later learned was really a creek) in search of frogs. Some days we might be brave enough to say aloud that we were hunting the feared water moccasins; these were the days that we were feeling particularly adventurous. Two small Black boys walking along the meandering stream out in the countryside. We had come a long way from trying to fish with a safety pin as the hook on the end of a long piece of twine. Fishing that way turned out to be a lot safer without an actual barbed hook. I'll never forget the time that I accidentally hooked Aunt Inee in the mouth just as I was about to cast my line. I was horrified by the sight of the worm thrashing about her bottom lip, unsure which was worse for her, the sharp hook that gouged her mouth or the slimy nightcrawler touching her lips. Either way, that misadventure was enough to stop me from fishing from that day on.

For the most part, I was a fearless hunter as a young boy . . . with one exception. The snakes didn't bother me nearly as much as did those blood-sucking leeches. On more than one occasion, I'd go racing home screaming at the top of my lungs at the sight of those engorged, slimy creatures that had firmly attached their mouths to my foot. I still don't know why time and time again I was foolhardy enough to pull off my shoes and socks to wade in the stream. My mother would calmly come out the back door with a saltshaker. Holding my leg steady to keep me from kicking her, she'd pour a pile of salt on each one until it would eventually give up and fall off my foot, leaving two small puncture wounds barely visible to the naked eye. I don't know if her former job as a candy striper or nurse's aide qualified her for this task, but the other customary operation she performed at least once each summer was to grab a pair of tweezers to extract a stinger out of my foot after I stupidly stepped on a honeybee.

While Greg's favorite weapons were his bow and the wide assortment of arrows that he bought as much for their exotic-looking points as for any belief in increased accuracy, mine was a plain old hand-me-down Daisy BB gun. This, despite an unpleasant incident one day that involved my brother firing his old BB gun while target practicing. The tiny BB ricocheted off the shed and struck me in the chest. I cried from fright more than real pain, but it reminded me once again that these things weren't toys to be carelessly handled. I wasn't particularly skilled at shooting an air rifle, but walking through the fields and along the creek gave me visions of big game hunting. Like the thrill of sneaking a peek and later actually touching my grandfather Lonnie's old single barrel ten-gauge shotgun that, for as long as I could remember, stood propped up against the wall just inside the cellar door. There was something about little boys and guns that seemed to define rural masculinity. It differed from what I imagined the relationship was for Black men from the city. Of course, there weren't many examples of those guys where I grew up, but I imagined they must have been something like my Uncle John.

My Aunt Ina's second husband, John Fredericks, was brought up in rural West Virginia, but he had what I might think of today as an urban-toughness veneer because of his quick temper, constant foul language, and his habit of cleaning his pistol for what seemed like hours on his never-finished back porch. "Rough around the edges" didn't quite describe him. He was an army veteran who had sandwiched serving in Italy during the Second World War between several years both before and after his time in the service laboring in the coal mines. You could see on him the effects of his decades of working in the coal-laden mountains and breathing in what passed for air in those days. While I had never heard of black lung disease, I had a strong sense that his persistent coughing and wheezing meant that there was something seriously wrong with him. He didn't go off to work each day like the other men in our family, noticeably different even for a kid to see. This John Henry Fredericks was nothing like his namesake. Instead of a chiseled body and powerful hammer in his hand, his was a broken-down frame with a beer bottle for an appendage. I don't ever recall seeing him without a cold Blatz in his hand or one sitting within easy reach, like a prosthetic that he took off to give his arm a momentary rest.

With his ever-present stocking cap pressed tightly down upon his head, I couldn't say for sure when the last time was that Uncle

John's slicked-back hair, often smelling of too much pomade, had been exposed to the air. Aunt Inee's discarded nylon stockings with their irrepressible, haphazard runs had been enlisted for years to tame what he called his nappies; although, I think that his constant use of her hose smashed his hair down into permanent rolling waves that reminded me of the ripples in the shallow portion of the creek. While he frequently treated his adopted son, my cousin, Bill, more harshly than I had ever experienced myself or seen other dads do to their sons, I guess he took a liking to me. More importantly, I wasn't afraid of him . . . even if maybe I should have been.

I couldn't have been more than five or six, but I recall one day when I found him crouching on his back porch watching for rats or other vermin down at the fence line separating his yard from the field. He carefully lifted up his shirt and pulled out his pistol from his right-back pocket. Then he touched his left index finger to his lips, motioning to me to remain silent as he slowly raised his right arm and squinted down the gun barrel. All of a sudden came a thunderous boom. The sound of the pistol discharging wasn't like that of a hunting rifle, something a bit more familiar when you live in the country, or even the muted *pow pow* that rang out from the television westerns that were nightly staples at my house. I was too young to understand how a noise like that could be both exciting and menacing all at the same time. "Shit," he'd say, "missed the damn thing." Then, with a smile that accentuated a pencil-thin mustache stenciled into his worn brown face, he beckoned me over to him. Placing the revolver into my right hand, he guided my arm up in the direction of a rusted metal barrel on the back of the property that spent many an evening with its contents ablaze. His pistol was much heavier than I thought it would be, nothing like the plastic and light metal toy guns that I had grown up with. He could barely insert his gnarled finger into the trigger over mine. I never knew if I was strong enough on my own to pull the trigger myself since the only thing I could feel was the pressure of his finger pulling mine back against cold steel. Now that I think about it, his taking aim to cock that gun was about the only time that his body seemed steady, and he was at least momentarily free of his hacking cough. The kick from the shot threw my arm up, and it's a wonder that it didn't cause me to shoot again, inflicting some real damage.

I'd practice my air gun marksmanship by shooting at torn-out magazine pages or the occasional outdated Sears-Roebuck catalog that I found in the odiferous "two-seater" outhouse in my grandmother's backyard. When I tired of blasting holes in the pages that I nailed up to the side of Grandma's outhouse, I'd climb through the fence and head down to the creek. Looking back, I realize that I wasn't a particularly enthusiastic hunter. While I appreciated that it took some skill to hit one's intended target, the problem for me was that those targets were alive. I should have known from those first few times that I managed to capture a minnow that eventually was left to die flopping in the grass that I wasn't cut out for this. My last foray as a hunter was only a few years later when I looked down the barrel of my new BB gun that I had selected as my reward for selling Christmas cards and seed packets. For youth tempted to become neighborhood solicitors, the value of the reward was in direct proportion to the amount of product that you sold. Since I had my eye set on a new air rifle, one of the pricier gifts, I really had to scramble going door to door pitching boxes of Christmas cards in the late summer and packets of seeds in winter, giving no mind to whether the women on my block felt any pressing need to purchase such things at that particular time of the year.

High in the tree above me on this day was a gray sparrow. Driven by the challenge of proving my growing confidence and skill, I took a steady aim, held my breath for an instant, and slowly pulled the trigger. The gun made a muted puff sound as the miniature bronze BB was pushed into the tree. Almost instantly I heard a muffled thump and saw the bird fall from the tree, its body hitting the ground just a few feet from where I stood. At first proud of my shooting skills, that feeling quickly changed to sadness as I saw the small lifeless creature, its eyes staring blankly up into the tree where it had usually found safety from threats on the ground. I don't know what happened to that air rifle. I can't remember if I ever used it again, haunted by that sickening feeling in my stomach that I had taken this bird's life for no good reason.

CHAPTER 17

INNOCENT CHILD'S PLAY

Summers seem to provide relief from more than just the winter blahs. The longer, warmer days were certainly welcome and always lifted the spirits. They also gave Oneida a bit of a break when the children could spend most of their time playing outdoors instead of being cooped up in our tiny house. And, of course, the utility bills came down when little or no gas was being used for heating. It stayed light out longer, which meant less electricity was needed. And everyone on the street had well water and a septic tank, although low water pressure meant that showers were for the most part nonexistent. Most importantly, it meant no water or sewer bills to pay. With the whole outdoors opened up to play, we had what seemed like our own veritable amusement park to explore, complete with tree houses that we built in the buckeye tree that rose tall from our backyard.

Each summer, furiously hammering nails with the purplish-brown hammer that was once my dad's, I'd often forget to watch out for protruding nails in the stray boards left carelessly lying around my construction site. At least once each year, a nail or two would find themselves positioned just so. And I would manage to step on it and feel it make its way up through the bottom of my tennis shoe, the steel sliding deep into my flesh. I'd let out a yelp that I'm sure could be heard over the entire block. I wasn't sure exactly what tetanus was, but I was scared half to death when my brother kept calling it lockjaw, puffing out his cheeks as if to demonstrate what happened when you lost control of your own face.

Summer nights on Miami Street were made for lying on beach towels or blankets in the backyard looking into the sky while waiting for the occasional shooting star. Aunt Inee had a partially broken pair of binoculars given to her by one of the families for which she worked. Just by hanging them around her neck, we were easily convinced that she could spot things that we couldn't. So, when she would raise them to her face and tell us that "that thing up there" was not an airplane, we believed her. Far too often impatient to stand with her in the yard for what felt like an eternity, we'd usually settle for a slow-moving jet way off in the distance, swearing that it was a flying saucer like the one that landed on the farm on that terrifying episode of *The Twilight Zone.* Even though the city folks who stayed over from time to time thought that country nights were darker than anything they had known, it seemed to me to be just the opposite. They were brilliantly illuminated with more stars than we could count along with a variety of other celestial objects that none of us could identify. And for much of the summer, the lightning bugs competed for our attention until all the kids in the neighborhood eventually relented by going in search of jars with lids. Carefully driving nails through the tops of the lids to make breathing holes, we'd place some grass in the jars and set out to capture a few dozen.

Running seemed to occupy a lot of our time. Running between the houses. Racing to be the first to the swings. Running up to the corner market before it closed to fetch something needed to prepare the evening's meal. Running in the field behind our house in pursuit of small animals that we had no chance of catching. Running away from hornet nests and snake holes. Running to catch our dog who managed to slip off the chain. On special nights, running to alert my grandmother to turn on her television; "Coloreds on," we'd yell as we banged on her screen door. We'd be running . . . just to run.

Summer days often meant endless adventures playing with cousins. My most cherished friend, and the person other than my mother, grandmother, and siblings that I probably loved more than anyone else in the world, was my closest cousin. Only three months younger than me, he was the person with whom I would spend hours each day just being curious kids. From catching frogs at the creek to building forts, we did it together. Playing tackle football, just the two of us, we pretended that we were on our favorite team, the Cleveland Browns. With limitless imaginations, our days were filled with the innocent wonder of childhood. But, that innocence was broken come one particular evening. It was in the nighttime during one of the sleepovers at my house that his real and horrible darkness was revealed to me. Much later, I came to understand that it was that darkness that my mother knew or suspected that caused her to forbid me to spend the night at his house.

My cousin would lie there and tell me stories, first quietly and then the pace of his pain-filled words would quicken with increasing anxiety in his eight-year-old voice. He spoke of being touched and made to touch others in places and in ways that children weren't meant to know or experience. He became even more upset as he relayed his feelings about the frequent, harsh discipline that he experienced at the hands of his stepfather, a Marine Corps veteran, who treated my cousin and his sister like noncompliant soldiers at basic training who needed to be taught a good lesson. One evening, while unburdening himself with these stories, he asked me to pray with him. Neither of us was particularly religious even though we occasionally attended Sunday school with our families. But his urgent need to pray was unlike anything that as kids we had experienced up to that point. Sure, we had knelt to say a goodnight prayer before, but never had we gotten out of bed after burrowing into the covers to do it.

We both got down on our knees, each of us beside one of the adjoining bunk beds in my tiny room and began to pray. At first, casually, we recited the familiar "Now I lay me down to sleep." Then, his tone became more serious, almost tortured. He asked God to save him, not from his sins but from awful things that "they" were doing to him. And, I was so shaken that I told God, in my pleading voice, that I wanted him to come down and rescue my cousin from the brutality and abuse in his life, even if I didn't know exactly what those things were, how to describe them, or what to call them. "Dear God," I prayed, "let him live in a good home like I do." And, then our hearts burst open, and the tears rolled down.

We began to sob almost hysterically. When my mother came into my room to find out what the commotion was about, all I could say was that we were praying and suddenly began to cry for no reason. She smiled as she comforted us, thinking that we were for the first time in our young lives caught up in the rapture of God. No, I didn't think so. We were grieving the loss of childhood innocence, even if my mourning the loss was happening vicariously. While my cousin's innocence had been stolen away from him long before this, I sensed that a part of mine was being taken as well. So, I feared his stepfather for his cruelty, like the time that he rubbed my other cousin's nose in her own feces when she had had an accident. He so mistreated my cousin's younger sister that she was eventually removed from their home and placed into foster care. To this day, I recall the time that he violently beat and then locked his wife, my oldest cousin, in a freezer to teach her a lesson. I despised that man for what he did to my best friend. I detested him for making his wife too afraid and unwilling to protect her own children, especially those who were not his biologically, from the monster that he was. Her neglect continued the cycle of abuse that so many in my extended family have experienced over the generations. To this day, my heart breaks for the many girls and boys in my family whose lives were tragically and irreparably broken by people they should have been able to trust to keep them safe. If ever we were saddled with a family curse, this could have been the one most likely to destroy us.

Even after the man's death some thirty years later, I couldn't look past that hatred and contempt that I felt for him. I couldn't bring myself to attend his funeral even if my refusal troubled my cousins, his widow, or the rest of the family. My stomach was turned by his presence as a pallbearer at my grandmother's funeral alongside my brother, cousins, and me. These cousins of mine who stood alongside me as pallbearers had at one or more times their own serious challenges, perhaps even what one might call tragic lives given their run-ins with the law and spending time in jail or prison. Yet, they all knew, I am sure, that they were loved by Grandma Hammonds despite their failings. But, it was ironic that this man would one day carry her casket given the fact that she had threatened to send him to an early grave if he stepped a foot onto her front porch in hot pursuit of his wife and her oldest granddaughter. Leveling Lonnie's old ten-gauge shotgun that was nearly as tall as she was, this diminutive woman had the look of a person willing to take it upon herself to avenge generations of abuse suffered by young girls and women in her family at the hands of heartless, evil men. While mustering a rage that was almost unrecognizable to her grandchildren, perhaps even to herself, she left no doubt that the violence was going to stop at her doorstep. There was no way on God's good earth that she could stand idly by and allow this shameful history to repeat itself under her roof. Not one more day, not one more minute, even if it meant giving up her ticket for a ride on that slow train to Jordan.

CHAPTER 18

INA MAE TO THE RESCUE

Fortunately for me, most of my childhood after I began school was largely free of conflict and tragedy. Mostly, I can recall life out in the country as simple and carefree. Looking back, I realize how much of those days were centered around food. Food wasn't just about culinary delights but a way of life. Meals were times for the families to come together and enjoy the outdoors. And what would summer be without backyard picnics and summer treats. Most of the time, the four or five households of family on our street would gather in my grandmother's yard for those "no special occasion" meals. And, man, would we eat . . . fresh picked corn on the cob, garden fresh beans and tomatoes. From time to time, we'd head over to one of the other houses where we'd engage in pulling taffy on Uncle Stan's front steps or hand-cranking an old ice cream maker on Uncle John's back porch while he slowly added a bag of ice to the outside of the bucket's base. It was an extra special treat when someone asked about getting a gallon of A&W root beer from the root beer stand just up the road; Aunt Mary was always more than willing to do it at the slightest suggestion. For those of us with a sweet tooth, I suppose that meant all of the children and most of the adults in the extended family, there was nothing better than Aunt Inee's homemade fudge.

Ina Mae Fredericks, the older of my mother's two sisters, was one of the most likeable people someone could ever meet, with an irrepressible kindness that seemed to ooze from her pores. Her sweetness was genuine, matched only by her extreme shyness, making it all the more distressing to think about the many personal hardships she had to endure over the years, much less to see her taken advantage of or mistreated. Some referred to her as the sister who got the short end of the stick when it came to the family's "pretty genes." She internalized those messages and remained self-conscious for much of her life about being heavier and darker than her younger sisters. Spending her entire adult life, and much of her adolescent years, as a maid left her constantly striving to please and care for others. She had worked for decades for a local doctor and his family as their housecleaner, cook, and caregiver. In many respects, she became the family's surrogate mother, and perhaps in some way the wife, as a stand-in of sorts for the Mrs. whose mysterious, chronic illnesses purportedly made it impossible for her to manage or contribute to the well-being of her family or household.

Rumor had it that the doctor's wife suffered from depression and alcoholism, and the latter would rear its ugly head during her periodic bouts of anger and surliness toward Ina. She seemed to resent my aunt for doing a much better job of keeping house and caring for the family than she was capable of. She also thought, even if it was just her imagination or the booze talking, that she caught her husband watching Ina go about her work around the house. What she thought she saw in his eyes made her furious. It was the type of gaze that she once knew and felt should be reserved for her, and her alone. While she hoped that he, known by most to be a very heavy drinker himself, would never stoop so low as to dishonor her, much less himself, by having a go at it with the help, it was painfully obvious to her that it had been longer than she could remember or was willing to admit that she had been a real wife to him. Still, she knew that without Ina's help that her family, her household, and, yes, even her marriage would likely have collapsed. She hated that her maid had this kind of power over her.

FIGURE 18.1. Oneida was especially fond of her older sister,
Ina Mae. A year after graduating from high school, she went to
West Virginia to live with Ina and her husband John.

Ina Mae was a devoted big sister to Oneida, one to whom my
mother was equally loyal. Only six years older than her younger sister, she had always felt a special responsibility to watch after Oneida,
especially after Sam's death. Building a simple, cinder-block house next
door was not just a coincidence; in fact, it turned out to be a godsend
when her baby sister was left to try to raise her family alone. Aunt Inee,
a big-bosomed bundle of smiles, was the ideal babysitter in a pinch
who could just fold you up into her arms and make you laugh even
before the tickling began. She'd let me crawl into her bed beside her on
the Friday nights that she watched me, chuckling all the while when I
pulled the sheets up over my head during the scary parts as we watched

Chiller Theatre and *The Twilight Zone* together on the small, fuzzy television set that was strategically placed opposite where she slept. When my mother returned from her evening out and called for me to come home, Aunt Inee would stand at the door as I made a mad dash to my house, intent on arriving safely before any monster could have its way with me during the ten-second sprint. On wet or snowy nights, I'd hit our concrete porch on a dead run and perilously slide into the metal porch furniture, frequently leaving bruises on the parts of my body into which I unceremoniously slammed.

And when things got serious, which they did on more than a single occasion, she was the first to be called when her little sister needed urgent help. I'm reminded of the time that my brother, Gregg, went into an epileptic seizure in the back of the car on the way home from church. Almost in a single motion, she snatched him up and forced a spoon wrapped in gauze into his mouth, an implement that she seemed to always have with her. In between her "Dear Jesuses" and "Help me Fathers," she repeated to herself over and over how she needed it in his mouth to keep him from biting off and swallowing his tongue. What a terrifying thought that was to me! She had learned from experience that the handy spoon was preferable to using her own fingers that she had nearly sacrificed in the process before. And when his eyes finally returned to their normal place, only moments before having frighteningly rolled back into his head, she would softly sing in a low voice all the while rocking back and forth as he slowly recovered. "He's got the whole world in his hands . . ." Her quick action became necessary on other occasions, including a few years later when Oneida's youngest child, Lori, was suspected of having idiopathic epilepsy. Running across the yard with the toddler in her arms and calling out for Ina between her frantic sobs, my mother was met by her sister at the door with one of the padded tongue depressors that she had spirited away from the doctor's office for just such an occasion. It surely was Ina Mae to the rescue.

CHAPTER 19

GEORGE HELPS HER MOVE ON

Like her mother, Oneida was considered by many to be a rather appealing widow. While there was no shortage of potential suitors, she was careful not to get involved with any man who couldn't see or agree to her putting her children first. It was one thing to step into the life of a woman who already had a few kids, but to have her directly say that her four kids would come first would often scare away those who had no intention of getting serious. The few men she allowed to come to our home and meet her kids were easily intimidated by our antics. Even though just kids, we seemed to like to put these guys through the wringer, usually at the instigation of the older two of us. We even sang a song about one of her intending male friends, Gene, who we nicknamed "Geno" because it fit into the parody of a commercial jingle for some household product that I don't recall. ". . . he's mean, and cruel, and bad, bad tasting—G—E—, N—O!"

There was one guy, however, who didn't get the business like the others did. There was something about him that made George seem different from the others. George was a gentle, pleasant man. Although we were still very protective of our mother, he slowly began to gain some trust with us. I was the first and easiest to win over since I was the youngest and, probably, most receptive to having a father figure in my life. I suspect that my two older siblings were steadfastly opposed to anyone coming into our mother's life. Nobody could replace our father, and, as far as they were concerned, he'd better not even try. Whereas, I had already told my second-grade classmates, after the teacher asked all of the children to say what their fathers did, that mine was a mail-man. Not exactly the truth, since she and George had not yet married, but it was too difficult to say that my dad was dead or to explain the nature of George's relationship to my mother and me.

George Lawson, upon discharge from the army, was one of the lucky ones; he obtained a job with the US Postal Service. Black men who landed federal jobs were extremely fortunate; the government paid better than most employers. It was fairly certain that it wouldn't go out of business, and most workers felt that they were fairly safe from being laid off. When Oneida met him, he was recently divorced and had two children of his own. He had been employed at the Columbus post office for nearly a dozen years, so there was ample evidence that he had a history of stable employment. That was important if she was going to think about a serious relationship with him or any man. As I got to know him better, it was easy to see how he won her over. He was kind, polite, and soft-spoken, pretty much the opposite of many of the men that she knew or had been around. He was, as she so often said to me, "a good guy."

Since George was also a World War II veteran, he was somewhat familiar with the vets benefit programs. Surprised that she hadn't been receiving VA survivors' benefits, he told Oneida that she should look into applying for assistance for herself and her children since he was aware that other widows of vets had been successful in applying for benefits. It wasn't until her oldest child was beginning to think about going to college that she realized that she needed to get serious about figuring out how the struggling family could afford that. No one in her family had ever gone to college before; most hadn't even graduated from high school. She knew nothing about how to apply to college and even less than nothing about how to put together the money if her kids decided that they wanted to go. So, all of the sudden she had to educate herself about the confusing world of college financial aid, especially since the high school guidance counselor wasn't accustomed to advising Black students about college resources.

The majority of the handful of Black students from Mt. Vernon who had gone to college went to Central State University, a historically Black state-run university that accepted any student who graduated from high school. That school routinely sought scholarships and received grants for its students so that college could be affordable for them while helping to keep the school afloat. Most of the students who attended came from households with modest incomes, if that, so aid counseling was a major priority for Black colleges. The staff at our town's high school seemed pretty much clueless at that time and didn't have much experience helping Black graduates get to college.

Oneida reached out to one of few Black persons in Mt. Vernon that she knew personally who had a college degree. Gilbert Newsom, a veteran of World War II, was the son of the former AME pastor who was a neighbor and had performed the wedding ceremonies for her sisters' marriages. Wilberforce University was founded by and administered by the African Methodist Episcopal Church and renowned as the training ground for many of the nation's most celebrated Black teachers going way back into the late 1800s. "Gib," as he was known, attended Wilberforce; its campus was only a mile away from Central State University, the state's other historically Black college or university situated in Xenia, Ohio.

After graduating from college, Gib Newsom returned to his hometown with a teaching degree in hand. To his disappointment, and that of the rest of the town's Black community, he was unsuccessful in gaining a teaching position in any of the local schools. He did, however, eventually land a job at Mt. Vernon High School when, needing work badly, he applied for the position of janitor. His hard-earned degree in hand was replaced by a broom and dustpan. And, he labored in the school's hallways in obscurity, cleaning the cafeteria and restrooms for years. In late summer of 1964, just before the school year began, the high school's industrial arts teacher resigned. Without time to search for his replacement, the principal was reminded that Mr. Newsom's degree and teaching certification qualified him for the job. After some discussion and little fanfare, the school board approved the hiring of its first Black teacher. That same year, prompted by the increasing calls for recognition of civil rights across the county, it hired Audrey Holt, another former resident who had grown up in the town, to teach in one of the system's elementary schools that fall as well. She became the first Black female teacher in the community.

What some who had college experience would consider to be among the simplest things proved confusing and difficult as Oneida tried her best to make sense of the college application process. She imagined that it must be like applying for a job; either you had the skills and they liked you or they didn't. No one told her or her oldest, Gregg, that many of the white students applied to several colleges hoping to be admitted to a few so that there would be a choice or at least a backup in case one's first choice didn't happen. If her son went to college, she just assumed that it would be to Central State like the handful of other Black children from Mt. Vernon fortunate enough to go to college had done. Now, she found herself trying to help him get to an unfamiliar college with which the high school band director had a connection and recommended to them. She had never even heard of Salem College, but if there was a chance for her son to get a badly needed scholarship, then that made up for the fact that his going to school in West Virginia would mean that he was going to be a long drive away from home.

Fortunately, Mr. Bechtel, the high school band director, took it upon himself to help Gregg figure out what he needed to head off to college. When the arrangements were complete in the summer of 1967, it became clear that he would be the first in Oneida's family to go to college. Both she and her mother gleamed; they only wished that Sam and Lonnie were around to witness it. When recalling those days, she later admitted to me that the tears she shed driving the four hours home after taking to him to school were as much about her pride that he would be doing what no one in the family had done before him as her sadness to be separated from her firstborn. Tears flowed again as she spoke about the hardships the family had faced to get to that moment, including Lonnie's passing, Sam's death, the pressure by her in-laws to break up her family, Gregg's epileptic seizures, and George's desire to move the family to Columbus.

CHAPTER 20

IT'S OKAY TO REMARRY

Oneida's remarriage gave her family some stability. Mostly, it gave a degree of financial security, something that she hadn't known since she was still living as a girl with her mother and Lon. It also brought another gift, a beautiful baby girl. After being the youngest for nearly 10 years, I was as happy as anyone to welcome a new sibling. They say that children in blended families can be brought closer together when one's parent and a new spouse have a child of their own. It is hard to imagine that our family could become closer than we already were. Some might say that our protective mother went overboard in shielding us from folks outside our family. At times, it did seem as though it was "us against the world." But there was no question that Lori's arrival was the greatest blessing to happen to us in a very long time, one that was long overdue and needed more than we could have possibly known. Newly remarried, Oneida knew that George wanted to move the family to Columbus where he worked. To appease him, she tried to muster enthusiasm about looking at houses, but she knew inside that it wasn't going to be easy to leave the house that she and Sam had built, as he always said, "for the kids." In the end, she convinced George that moving would mean enrolling the children in the city schools that were already reputed to be far inferior to the schooling that her kids had access to from the start. She also thought that those

FIGURE 20.1. Before George entered her life, it had been a long time
since Oneida found herself laughing and having fun with a man.

schools would be more dangerous, remembering her experiences visiting her friend Sue.

Oneida wasn't happy that George had planned to keep his efficiency
apartment on the city's east side, at least, he said, until they moved the
family to Columbus. While it was true that his commute for work
was taking its toll, so was her concern that he was still living, at least
part of the time, like a bachelor. The friendly, elderly landlady from
whom he rented the second floor Monroe Avenue apartment took a
liking to Oneida. While she was fond of George and liked having this
polite, courteous young man as her tenant, she made it known that she
thought it was a bad idea for him to continue to rent her space once he
remarried. She never said exactly why, but I assume that Mrs. Jackson,
George's kind but protective landlady could tell that it was the source
of one of the couple's biggest blowups. I had never seen my mother so
mad at George before, even when he drank too much, as he so often

did. This time, the argument was different, punctuated by her piling his shoes and clothes on the front porch. It shocked and worried me greatly to hear her cursing and throwing things at him.

George had a serious, but generally unacknowledged, drinking problem, probably going back to his days in the service. Unlike other alcoholics who became belligerent and argumentative, he tended to simply fall asleep . . . in chairs, on the couch, or even stretched out on the floor. He enjoyed having company when he drank, so our house was often the place for other serious drinkers. His friend Bill was one of the drunks with a temper who was around much more than any of us cared to have regularly in our home; his drinking would often result in a big argument. Invariably, he and his wife, Anita, would eventually cuss each other out and come to blows. I recall as a teenager becoming so upset by their constant fighting that I shouted from my bedroom, "Shut the fuck up!" Me, the quiet teenager who had never even uttered the comparatively tame "damn it" in my parents' presence. I disliked this man with a passion and couldn't find myself having sympathy for his wife. It didn't make sense to me that she stayed with that asshole.

I was always grateful that I never saw or heard my stepfather, George, strike my mother, nor did I ever suspect that he had done so when I was not around. I never even heard him curse back despite the verbal barrage that she could unleash. Still, it was clear that something would have to change if they intended to stay married. Since their daughter, Lori, was growing up pretty much like an only child after all of her older siblings had graduated from high school and moved away before she was even barely in grade school, that would have seemed to have been the opportunity for the family to move to the city. George would no longer have the hour commute, something that resulted in him totaling his car after hitting a deer and spending a weekend in jail after he was charged and convicted of driving under the influence. Yet, the tug of the house on Oneida's heartstrings just wouldn't go away; in some ways, it was stronger than ever. In the end, they decided to remain in the house, and George continued to drive the fifty miles to work at 5 a.m. each morning. Staying put in Mt. Vernon was both good and bad for them. Perhaps, it was an advantage for Lori, being so much younger than her siblings. For the most part, she didn't have to go through school with teachers who had taught and known her brothers and sisters and deal with constantly being compared to them. A disadvantage, as far as the family went, was that we had so few common experiences as children or adolescents. There wasn't any overlap between our teen adventures and hers. So, we settled for watching her grow up from afar. The major disadvantage was the missed opportunity for our youngest sister to grow up and live in a significantly more diverse community. It is hard to imagine how different her life would have been from ours had she attended schools with people who looked like her and been around people who affirmed her identity as a Black person.

Still, George served in many ways as our family's gateway to urban African American life and culture. Although born in Florida and raised by relatives in Connecticut, he had been living for a decade and a half in the predominantly Black, segregated neighborhoods of Columbus before he met our mother. After his stint in the army, the choice regarding where to live when he settled in Ohio's capitol city wasn't really his. He and his first wife, Gwen, had attempted to purchase a house on the mostly white north side of town but were denied loans repeatedly through a lending practice that later became known as redlining. Eventually, they and other Black couples became part of a class action lawsuit against some realtors and their complicit lending companies. While the government claimed to put a stop to that discriminatory practice when it signed a consent order with the guilty parties, it was apparent that Columbus remained markedly segregated for decades.

Our occasional forays to Columbus' near east side and the less frequent visits of George's Black post office co-workers to our home out in the country were filled with intrigue. The city-based BOSEA men's club, whose membership was comprised of what seemed at the time to be upwardly mobile Black men, would meet each summer at our house. The little town in which we lived just didn't have folks like these, or so it seemed. The way they talked and the way they seemed to effortlessly have a grand old time was like nothing that I had seen before. Sometimes, I was sure that how much fun one had was measured in decibels. My experience was that Black folks from the city were loud. While our white neighbors stomped their way through country and western line dancing, George and his friends introduced us to the Madison. As soon as the right music began to play, Black folks gathered on the dance floor to glide through the steps with the widest grins one could imagine. Sure, our white friends played cards, too, but their relatively tame euchre games were no match for a rancorous game of bid whist. It was fascinating as a child to watch the whist victors, sweat pouring from their brows, jump to their feet and slam their card down hard on the card table as they crowed about their virtual invincibility.

Eating was always at the center of family events and social occasions in rural Ohio, but our usual fried chicken and potato salad staples were tame compared to the pork-derived offerings that George introduced in our household. In addition to bringing around foods that were new to us, this man also seemed to enjoy cooking as well. I can still see the gallon-sized jar of pickled pigs' feet and a bag or two of pork rinds that he brought home with him from work, usually with a pound and a half of fresh perch from Ray Johnson's fish market that he made a special trip downtown to procure. When he got home, he'd immediately place what the market claimed was the "catch of the day" in a cornmeal batter and drop the filets into a pan filled with hot oil. The unmistakable aroma of fried fish wafted throughout the house and was immediately mixed with a nostril-opening shake from the bottles of Louisiana hot sauce or Tabasco that always came out on such occasions.

But it was the pork entrails that caused the greatest stir, an equal measure of both enthusiasm and repulsion. Even the name "chitlins" sometimes sounded humorously close to one of our primary concerns about eating a pig's boiled intestines. Occasionally, one of us would be bold enough, outside the presence of grownups, to pronounce them with the "s-h" beginning sound that struck us as both funny and appropriate. And, yet, there was something oddly compelling to be eating what we imagined to be a common source of meat, if you want to call it such, that our enslaved ancestors had to consume to survive. Still, our mother would spend hours at the sink scraping and scratching endlessly at the weird looking casings, determined to eliminate any trace of foul residue. She would frequently remind us that "you just don't eat chitlins after any old body; they don't clean them like I do. They're not as particular." And, if we had friends over to our house when chitlins were being cooked, we'd first have to explain what the awful smell was and, secondly, make it a point to tell them that the spelling on the five-pound bucket—"chitterlings"—was probably done that way for white people to know what they were but was definitely wrong. Everybody knew that there was no "er" when it came to those things.

My youth, like that of my older siblings and so many of my peers, was marked by the events and issues of the day. As teenagers coming of age in the '60s and early '70s, there was no shortage of those, especially for young people of color living in a predominantly white, rural area in Ohio. From the assassination of President John F. Kennedy (ruining my sister Karen's thirteenth birthday) through the murder of Dr. Martin Luther King Jr. (shattering all of our hearts), we were affected. With the shooting of students on the campuses of Kent State University (and Jackson State University, which was rarely mentioned in the news nor memorialized in song by Crosby, Stills, Nash and Young), we struggled to find our places in society.

Some people in our little town suggested that the Sheffield family seemed to benefit from some type of special status in the way that we were treated and perceived in our community. While it is hard to attribute any of our accomplishments or opportunities, like my sisters being selected for high-profile positions as majorettes and court attendants, to favoritism, they may have been perceived as such by a few of the other Black students and their parents who were quick to tell people that we thought we were better than everyone else. Petty jealousies existed in every community, but they stung even more when they came from within a group that was already extremely small. It was painful at times feeling like an outsider within the community with which you identified and, maybe even sought acceptance, the most.

Even though we were geographically removed from larger Black communities, we were not unaffected by the injustices experienced by Black people in America. We just had fewer venues to express it. We began adopting Afro hairstyles in the late sixties and early seventies, something that was frowned upon by the older colored folks as well as the white community. Debi, selected the school's Forum Queen in 1971, was told that she would not be permitted to wear a natural hairstyle at the show. She wore a wig that was unceremoniously tilted to the side as if to protest the unfairness. Because there were few Black students in her class and interracial couples were frowned upon, she asked a Black friend's brother from an adjoining town to be her escort for the ceremony. The high school was willing to deviate from the customary practice of having escorts enrolled in the home school so as to avoid the problem of her being escorted by a white boy. She reciprocated by offering me as her friend's escort for a similar event at her rural school. It was a strange experience sitting on the Centerburg High School stage with her friend Sheila, surrounded by students I had never before met or even seen. My participation in this awkward sibling exchange reminded me of how clearly the color line was defined and enforced in our rural schools.

In our small town, where white residents were quick to claim that racial prejudice was not a problem, it couldn't have been further from the truth. Due to our small numbers, they just couldn't see it . . . or refused to. I suspect that for many white people, those types of memories are fairly short and most times faulty. For Black folks, they last a lifetime, living on as part of a cultural heritage that serves to help keep you safe and remind you not to let your guard down. The older Black folks had learned these lessons well. Sometimes, they came more gradually to the young folks. But they always came. It's like the times that white people said *nigger* in your presence, but they "didn't mean you."

Like many Black male students in Mt. Vernon, I played sports. One of the most vivid memories that I have from my days on the junior high school basketball team epitomized the isolation of being the "only one" on my team. As an eighth grader, I sat in the bleachers with my teammates watching the seventh-grade team play its game just before my team played. Our school's two teams traveled to games together, and the older players sat behind our younger team's bench during their game and vice versa. As we watched, a Black player from Coshocton, oddly enough another small town with few Black residents and, by chance, my mother's birthplace, proceeded to "school" players on Mt.

Vernon's younger all-white team. As he darted around and through our school's team, he seemed to score at will. Exasperated and annoyed, a teammate of mine sitting just three seats away screamed out, "Stop that nigger!" On the bus ride home from the game, I sat silently by myself. After arriving back at the school, and before I got to my mother's car, two of my teammates came up to me and apologized for what the other had said. I pretended that I hadn't heard it. They were surprised but clearly relieved, never realizing that I wasn't able to admit to having been hurt by what my own teammate had said that afternoon.

It's funny, but nearly three decades later that memory came crashing back into my life when I sat in the bleachers watching my eighth-grade daughter participate in a track and field event at her school. Sitting just a few rows behind me in the stands were students speaking fairly loudly about who knows what. What was easily heard was one of the students expressing frustration and concern that my daughter's team would have to face a Black sprinter on the other team. "Don't worry," one said. "Our nigger will beat their nigger." My daughter was the only Black runner from her team on the track that afternoon. When I turned around to see who was being so insensitive, I was hurt to see that all three of the students were wearing Mt. Vernon track uniforms. They were my daughter's teammates! But, I was no longer in eighth grade and incapable of speaking up. I rose and walked straight over to the coach, who I had known for a couple of years because of my children's sports activities. After being told what I had heard, she called the students over and immediately threatened to dismiss them from the team. Intervening, I told her that I didn't want them thrown off the team but would rather have them come out to the college where I was teaching to join my students and me in a discussion of the significance of race in American society, even small towns. Although they agreed to do it as a way to stay on the team, none of them ever came to my class.

CHAPTER 21

I GOTTA GET OUT OF HERE

Nineteen sixty-eight was a difficult year for all of Black America; it was especially difficult for those of us living in small towns, despite what many in this country assumed. In April of that year, I recall a school official coming into my classroom and whispering to the teacher at the front of the room. As her face flushed, she breathlessly announced to the class that civil rights leader "Martin King" had just been shot and killed. I was every bit as stunned as one of my classmates seemed elated. An enormous lump rose in my throat as I watched him nearly leap from his seat to rejoice upon hearing the news. I didn't let on how hurt I was that he could celebrate the death of a man in whom I had placed so much hope. I couldn't show how deeply crushed I felt at that moment, perhaps partly due to his thoughtless insensitivity. Dr. King's messages of peace and justice stirred me to my soul, giving me reason to believe that things could get better for people like me.

I suspect that it was at that moment on that fateful day in April of 1968 that I knew that I had to get out of Mt. Vernon. It was abundantly clear that none of my classmates understood why I was so invested in Dr. King; none could feel my pain. I had reached the point where the alienation that I felt from my childhood friends and former classmates was palpable. While I was moving forward and coming to understand more deeply, more personally what race in America meant, they were content in believing that Mt. Vernon didn't have any race problems. I can almost hear them now, "What was all the fuss about?" I knew that I had to leave that small town as soon as humanly possible. I felt then that I would never return or, at least, never live there again. As I grew older, I came to realize that my classmate's reaction to Dr. King's slaying was somewhat understandable given how the civil rights leader had been villainized in the press during a time that the FBI and others tried to discredit him. As a consequence of a massive disinformation campaign, he was seen by many white people, not just those in small towns, as a troublemaker and rabble-rouser. So, I came to view that high school episode as emblematic of America's racial divide, one that would not be easily reconciled, especially in small towns like the one that I felt compelled to leave. Years later, a former classmate inquired of me why I never attended our high school reunion. When I told her that it wasn't a very pleasant time in my life, she indicated that she was surprised to hear that. She said, "You were always so popular and well-liked, and a really good basketball player." My response was simply, "I guess you really didn't know me back then, did you?" She apparently had forgotten what a stink her friendship with me had caused in her own family. Another classmate later told me that this girl's father had once made it abundantly clear that I was never to be her friend.

White people generally seem to have trouble seeing or certainly beginning to understand how often and much Black people have experienced racial discrimination and prejudice throughout American society. White people in rural communities throughout the North in particular have had an especially difficult time confronting or even admitting that racism existed in their towns. The fact that restaurants in Mt. Vernon were known to and, in fact, did not serve Black customers is something that most white people cannot believe or would prefer not to believe. As a teenager, I was told and came to learn firsthand that Black people were not welcome in many of the town's private clubs and civic organizations; those attitudes extended to public spaces that on their face probably appeared to locals as being at worst indifferent to, even if not desirous of, our patronage. There was a reason that we didn't swim at the Sunset Club or feel welcome at the local

Community Pool. No one wanted to hear how Mike Duckworth, the only Black swimmer on the YMCA's swim team, wasn't permitted to compete when the opposing team's coach and parents objected. Few were willing to see how it was a common practice throughout Ohio to maintain segregation at swimming facilities even when the pools were funded by taxpayers' dollars.

The fact that Black youth would roller skate on a specific night of the week at Mt. Vernon's roller rink and travel to other small towns to skate on other nights was lost on white folks in our town. "Colored night," as it was called, was the designated skating time set aside each week for Black youth to enjoy the popular pastime that white teenagers could just assume was available to them whenever they wished. Generations of Black youth in small towns throughout the area learned to skate in segregated rinks. Skating reached the height of its popularity in our town from about the 1940s through the 1960s. More than just a fun pastime, it was also a venue in which to meet other Black people when they would travel to Mt Vernon to roller skate. A few of those social outings resulted in courtships, and local girls like Dian Hammonds and Mary Carter eventually met their future husbands at the skating rink. Sadly, few, if any, of the persons still living today know or remember that Black people gained the right to skate in this town after a lawsuit was filed under a newly enacted state civil rights statute against the rink's owner back in the 1880s. Things weren't all that different ninety years later, especially in small-town America.

The high-profile deaths in 1968 of the Reverend Dr. Martin Luther King Jr. and the liberal Senator Robert F. Kennedy stunned the nation. These tragedies confirmed for Black Americans that racial justice and the quest for civil rights were even further from reality than we had feared. In a country where the lives of African Americans have never been valued as much as those of white people, the killing of a Black person at the hands of a white person has been so common that it has rarely come as a surprise. From highly publicized killings like that of young Emmett Till to local or regional disappearances that few would acknowledge and about which no one would comment, racial violence against people because of the color of their skin had always been a part of the world in which we lived.

There were some in my family whose memories of life in Virginia were fresh enough to recall the fear of being killed. It seemed to fester like a sore that would never heal. And when we became impatient and picked off the scab, it always reminded us of the underlying wound and the permanent scar that we would undoubtedly carry with us for the rest of our lives. As June Edwards use to say to his daughter Bertha, "We're just a fast, long-legged dog and a box lunch away from how things were back home." It was his way of reminding her that we weren't all that far removed from sitting in the back of that Greyhound bus heading north. So, whatever relief he felt as the bus rumbled across the bridge high above the Ohio River on the return trips from visiting family down south, he knew that it wasn't just down there that colored folks needed to stay vigilant. I suppose that it wasn't a coincidence that the bus station in Mt. Vernon was situated for a time almost directly across the street from the local AME church, the county's first Black congregation. Many a Black migrant who journeyed to this small town in central Ohio reached their destination, both literally and spiritually, from the back seat of an exhaust-filled fifty-seat carriage.

When tragedies did occur in small-town America, where most would assume residents are free from that kind of harm, they tended to impact the lives of all of us who felt at risk in an environment where we easily stood out. Deaths by violence touch both families and communities. There is no question that the killing of my Uncle Herman caught our whole family, if not the entire community, off guard. While the loss of loved ones is a natural part of life, how they depart can speak volumes about the world in which they live and shape people's view of that world. The cultural memories of Black people, even those living in rural Ohio, are filled with stories of racial injustices. The most terrifying and paralyzing involve acts of violence. It was just such an event that touched my family on the 23rd day of March 1968, less than two weeks before Dr. King's assassination.

Our cousin, Norma Jean Edwards, Uncle Herman and Aunt Eva's only daughter, was by all accounts a typical young woman living in the rural Appalachian hills of Ohio. In 1967, she was a recent graduate in Belmont County's Barnesville who had dated the same boy through much of high school. Like many girls in those parts, she hoped to marry and have children of her own one day, sooner as opposed to later if she had her way. Her being mixed-race didn't change her aspirations in that regard the least bit; she didn't think that her being one-quarter Black would make that much difference. After all, to look at her, most people wouldn't have even guessed. Only her last name, Edwards, identified her in the community as being a colored girl, or "part-colored" as her white mother would say. When the day came that her longtime boyfriend, Bill, proposed to her, she couldn't have been happier. The only problem was that his widowed mother wasn't fond of Norma Jean; in fact, she had tried time and again to discourage the relationship. She was determined that her son was not going to marry "one of them." When her son refused to listen after she told him he was forbidden to see the girl and discouraged by her lack of success in breaking up the couple, she would spend hours, sometimes days, holed up in her house fretting and crying uncontrollably. Billie told Norma Jean that his mother would eventually come around, especially if she had grandkids that she could fuss over and spoil.

Norma Jean began to make plans to get married. She knew that there would be no lavish wedding. Uncle Herman, her 65-year-old semi-retired father, was a part-time scrap dealer living on social security and whatever additional money he could scrape together when he went junkin'. So, there wasn't any money for a big wedding even if her parents had wanted to pay for a fancy affair. Eventually, the young couple began to consider whether a trip to the courthouse for a quick civil ceremony was the best that they could hope for. Besides, it could happen sooner so they could start their lives together right away. On March 23rd, Norma Jean and nineteen-year-old Bill made plans to travel with their parents to the courthouse to apply for a marriage license.

Herman, Eva, and their daughter arrived around 9:30 that morning to pick up the girl's fiancé and his mother, Pauline Porter. The short drive to the courthouse in St. Clairsville wouldn't take long; perhaps they would have a nice lunch at the Newellstown Diner. When they pulled into the driveway, Pauline seemed agitated but remained unusually silent. Over the past couple of years, she increasingly appeared older and more haggard than a woman of forty-one would have been expected to look; the loss of her husband to a heart attack had taken its toll. After getting into the back-passenger side of Herman's car, she told her son that she had forgotten her wallet and asked him to retrieve it. After Bill entered the house, his mother reached into her purse and pulled out a gun. In the blink of an eye, there was a flash from the .38 caliber pistol that was nearly twice the size of her hand. Uttering something about how she couldn't allow this to happen, she shot Herman four times in rapid succession. Then, she turned the gun on Eva, who was leaning over to help her dying husband, shooting her twice.

Before his mother could shoot his hysterical fiancé, Bill pulled Norma Jean from the car and stood between them. Begging Pauline to give up the gun, Bill told his mother that she'd have to shoot him to get to the girl. When she put the gun back in her purse, Bill quickly took the bag from her. He rushed Norma Jean into the house and called the authorities. When the sheriff arrived, Pauline had returned to her house, cutting her hand trying to break in to finish the job. The law enforcement report indicated that she offered no resistance when she was taken into custody; she was eerily calm in the face of all the carnage.

According to the coroner, Herman and Eva died instantly. The autopsy report released to the paper stated that the cause of death for both victims was certain. They died of gunshot wounds to the head. His body was found slumped over against the driver-side car door with both hands still clutching the steering wheel. Her body was next to his in the middle-front seat just as she often preferred to ride. Although indicted for murder, Pauline Porter was found not competent to stand trial. Eventually, she was committed to a mental hospital, where she remained until her death. While Norma Jean and Bill did eventually marry, the tragedy was more than their ill-fated marriage could survive.

In 1968, I was a high school freshman. That time in my life remains a blur for me, not that it went by quickly. On the contrary, it seemed to drag on forever, as if the years had been extended by double the usual time. My alienation from my white classmates and teammates became more pronounced. They couldn't understand "why the Negroes were rioting" or what they hoped to achieve by "all those marches." My shyness wouldn't allow me to shout out loud what I was feeling, and my fearfulness kept me from acting out. I would sit at home in my room for hours in search of consolation from James Brown. "Uh, wid ya badd self. Say it loud. I'm Black and I'm proud." First with the volume down low, and slowly over the evening bringing the volume up as I played his anthem over and over until my mother had to tell me to "turn that record down." I wanted an Afro so badly that, like my older sisters, I washed my hair repeatedly in Axion and Tide detergents to get my hair to nap up enough for an artificially achieved "natural" look. I became one of the first Black students in my high school to wear a "Fro," to the chagrin of my basketball coach, who had previously taught at another school with more Black students. He purportedly wasn't liked very well by any of them. I wasn't sure which he liked less, the way I wore my hair or the fact that my girlfriend was white.

High school was difficult enough for young people who were as shy as me. When race was brought into the picture, it was at times especially hard. My becoming extremely self-conscious was likely the result of a deadly combination of cultural insecurity and personal introversion. For the most part, my social life vacillated between occasionally attending high school dances at the Y, where I often stood off to the side and watched others dance, or whatever they called what they were doing out on the dance floor, and staying at home to listen to music in my tiny bedroom. Starting in junior high school, then later in high school like many of the guys, I had developed crushes on a couple of girls who, after a couple of awkward phone calls, informed me that their parents told them that I wasn't to call them again. Given that there was only one Black girl in my entire graduating class, they didn't have to explain to me why. I knew the drill well after watching my brother try to navigate resistance to his dating a couple of white girls who were in the high school marching band with him. By then, I had come to know all of the words to Bobby Taylor and the Vancouvers'

"Does Your Mama Know About Me." I assume that it was my brother who bought the 45-rpm single that got played at my house time and time again.

When the Vancouver's song came out in 1968 in the midst of the Black Pride movement, it was ironic, but not surprising, that more than half of the Black guys in the high school were dating white girls. In rural towns like ours, there was little choice, except to be alone. Each attempt to do what other male teenagers were doing was accompanied by worries about the parents of the girl who caught your eye. The lyrics of the song tumbled around in my mind often as I wondered what they would say when they found out that the guy on the other end of the phone was Black. It didn't take long to find out, and it became a common refrain throughout high school. Having white parents assume, if not outright say, that you weren't good enough for their daughters because of your race was difficult. It happened time and time again. Having seen racial insensitivity and resistance about interracial dating in my own family result in violence and death, I knew that things could get even worse. And as a parent of two sons, my mother had good reason to worry about our well-being. I just didn't know that it began the moment that we were moving about our neighborhood outside her watchful eye. Even as a first-grader, I got a taste of my mother's fear, although at the time I didn't understand why my giving a school friend, Pammy, a ride home on my new Schwinn bicycle that my mother had purchased at the local Western Auto for my sixth birthday, was an issue. It was clear that this otherwise innocent act between grade schoolers left my mother worried about my safety. Pam chatted with excitement, her long, yellow-blonde hair blowing in the wind, as I pedaled swiftly down the street. How my mother learned that Pam's parents objected to our childhood friendship escaped me. But, I know that it didn't help that my mother was painfully aware of the close call with being lynched that Grandpa Edwards had or even the more recent incident in 1955 when a young Black teenager, Emmett Till, lost his life because of the baseless fears of a white woman.

The obsession with racial purity was coupled with an often-repeated rallying cry from white men to protect "white womanhood." Included among the avowed guardians were many men who routinely abused and disrespected the very women that they claimed to be championing. Rural communities up north were not immune from these deeply held racist attitudes, especially those grounded in the fear of race mixing. Even in a state like Ohio that no longer had an anti-miscegenation law, the actions of white folks aimed at enforcing the social codes that punished Black men who dared to have relationships with white women remained strong. What at times could look like tolerance, even if not acceptance, of interracial couples in many, if not most, small towns was often the consequence of relatively small numbers and intentional strategies that reduced their visibility to the extent that maintaining a low profile and limited visibility could have been possible. When my brother and I came of age to begin dating, Oneida's concern seemed to take on a whole new dimension. The death of her Uncle Herman in 1968 was tragic enough. The killing of her mother's brother and his wife because of an interracial relationship just added fuel to the fire.

One girl who had shown interest in me in 1970 was the daughter of a local college professor. After our exchange of a few phone calls, she told me one evening between sobs and her anguished apologies that she had been forbidden by her father to see me. She found out almost immediately that he wouldn't be understanding as she had believed. She was devastated by his intervention and deeply resentful of the clear hypocrisy of her father professing social equality in his public posturing while forbidding his daughter to have a relationship with a Black guy. This was made even worse for her because he was known at the college as a social liberal who had even supported the formation of the county's chapter of the NAACP. And, he wasn't the last to tell his daughter that a friendship with me was out of the question. It was ironic when I moved to Gambier and began teaching at Kenyon College that I had become a neighbor and colleague to a couple of these men, whom I am certain would have vehemently denied having ever told their daughters that they were not allowed to date me.

CHAPTER 22

IF NOT FOR BAD LUCK, HE'D HAVE NO LUCK AT ALL

I rode a motorcycle in high school, a pretty daring thing for someone who was naturally timid and didn't want to stand out. The vulnerability experienced on a bike isn't just physical because of the danger of wrecking; it comes with and requires, to a large extent, a frequent invasion of one's personal space. Your body is fully visible when it isn't encased in metal like it is when moving in a car. It wouldn't take much for someone to reach out and actually touch you . . . or spit on you. It would take even less effort to call you names or threaten you. Yet, there was a sense of freedom that drew me to motorcycles; perhaps, it was the opposite of what I was feeling during my school days. Even after suffering my first and only wreck, seeing myself in what felt like slow motion flying over the handlebars and sliding across the pavement, I wasn't deterred from riding despite the holes burned in my leather jacket and the bubble shield on my helmet. I couldn't imagine what my face would have looked like had it made direct contact with the road without the protection of that clear plastic face shield.

Yet, that motorcycle helped me cope. I was always so composed in class; always in control while playing sports. I'm not sure that I knew what a stoic was, but I definitely knew how to perform the part. But zipping down the highway, especially at night, gave me a strange sensation of tranquility at the same time that I was experiencing a rush of

adrenalin. For once in my life, I didn't feel so constrained. I even met
a girl who later would become a love interest because of our motorcycles. Seeing her often when she parked in the designated spot for
motorcycles, I was clearly intrigued. She had moxie. When she took
her helmet and sunglasses off, it was also clear that she was absolutely
drop-dead gorgeous. I'm sure that it was she who spoke first and initi-
ated a conversation; I was much too shy to have done so. Given that
she was one of the prettiest girls in my high school, I couldn't even
begin to imagine that she might find me the least bit interesting, let
alone "cute" as they called it back then. I still see images in my mind of
our motorcycles parked next to each other, almost touching at times.

Motorcycle riding ended for me about a decade later; for her, about
the same time . . . after we had married and both graduated from our
respective law schools. In the intervening years, we learned a lot about
ourselves and each other. Some of the discoveries and lessons were
hard, if not heartbreaking. Many of the most difficult ones revolved
around race: me trying to find my place in a polarized world; and she,
I was certain, not understanding how conflicted I was. It was more
than just cultural alienation; it was at times full blown existential angst.
Who the hell was I? Who and what did I want to be? It was a bad
time for anyone going through all that shit to be in a serious relationship. It was even worse because it began at such a young age and
extended through the years when most young people would be trying
on identities like a new change of clothes. One's public face should be
sufficiently malleable when you are young to quickly start over again
and apply new makeup when the mood or situation arises. Unless, you
are too insecure and uncertain about what that face looks like to others . . . not just some people, but everybody. It was like being back in
elementary school and determined not to mess up. And, for the most
part, I didn't.

I dreaded messing up because I knew that the consequences could
last a lifetime. One of the primary lessons I had for this was my cousin
Bill. Bill Fredericks was the adopted son of my mother's sister Ina and
her second husband, John. I hadn't realized it or thought much about
the fact that for much of his younger life he went by the name "Billy

King." Now, it makes sense to me that he had another last name before he was officially adopted and explains why he was enrolled in our elementary school under that name. I just assumed that his life as a child was pretty much like that of my siblings and me, even though the reality for many adoptees can be quite the opposite. From the small things to the not so small, I believe that B. B., as he came to be known, was treated quite differently. Not that his adoptive parents didn't love him, as I'm sure that they did, but they had a very different way of showing it from what I had experienced.

Living with a very strict father and a submissive, abused mother meant that Bill heard and witnessed conflict that I never knew. Based upon the yelling that I heard coming from the house next door, he was sometimes also the subject of cruel criticism and belittling. As best I could tell, Bill wasn't a particularly strong student, but he wasn't "stupid," as my Uncle John often called him. Nor was it true that he couldn't do anything well as he was repeatedly told. By high school, it became quite clear that Bill could do something well . . . very well indeed. He could run like the wind. The first inkling was as children dashing around the neighborhood, running through backyards and racing home from school. No one beat him, and he seemed to be able to run forever and with ease. So, as a high school cross-country and track runner, he was one of the best. He won several competitions and repeatedly established new times and records seemingly at will. The trophies, ribbons, and medals quickly multiplied. We all just knew that he would become a track star in college and make a name for himself.

During the fall of 1966, in his senior year of high school, Bill continued to impress on the cross-country courses with his smooth stride, gliding effortlessly from start to finish. Things at home, however, weren't going as well. His father, long suffering from a respiratory disease, was declining. Eventually, his parents turned their tiny, cramped living room into the closest thing to a hospital room that one could imagine. Uncle John spent nearly all of his time between the pullout sofa and the tiny bathroom just a few steps away, eventually becoming so weak that he took his meals in bed. With Aunt Ina working her regular job as housekeeper, cook, and babysitter for a doctor's family, Bill was expected to take some responsibility for tending to the needs of his ill dad. And, Uncle John didn't make it easy. Between his wheezing and coughing, he managed to find enough breath to try his damnedest to yell belittling insults at Bill and remind him "just who the man of the house" was, even if he, in a chronic invalid state, could barely get himself up off the couch if he had wanted to teach his son a lesson. Running became as much an escape from the tension and constant conflict in his house as it was shaping up to be a potential avenue for life after high school.

In the late 1960s, colleges and universities were being challenged to make themselves accessible to African American students. Many took the route of recruiting and admitting promising Black athletes who could contribute to their sports programs. Bill found himself getting attention from college track coaches. It was all a very heady affair for him to have someone saying they really wanted him. At the same time, it was frightening. For a young man who had suffered his whole life from low self-esteem, he received the college attention as another source of stress. He had struggled academically throughout his school years; what made him now think that he could make it through college? His father had left school before graduating from high school, and his mother had done the same. They proved to be no help in thinking about his options; to the contrary, they echoed his own doubts about whether he was cut out to do it.

Despite the letters from a handful of colleges, including an offer of admission and scholarship from Malone College, he had become convinced that they didn't know who they were recruiting. They didn't understand how unprepared he was, or at least he felt, for college. And attending Malone where a former high school girlfriend and a former track teammate were enrolled terrified him. What if they would be there to witness him fail? During a visit to that school, he was convinced by his own fears that going there wouldn't work. Eventually, he told himself the same thing about all of the others as well. He convinced himself that he was pretty lucky to have landed a decent-paying factory job, so, as the saying goes, "a bird in the hand . . ." Having opted not to go to college, time passed more slowly than usual. At

FIGURE 22.1. Ric (L) looked up to his cousin Bill (R), who was popular,
a gifted athlete, and maintained a modest demeanor.

least, he thought, if he moved out of the house, he could finally be his
own man.

Everyone knows that the late 1960s was the time of experimenta-
tion, and my cousin Bill seemed to be as attracted to and excited by
the generational sirens of sex, drugs, and alcohol as anyone. A couple
of major problems for him, though, were that he was more than just
a little attracted to this life, and he was a Black man living in a predominantly white rural town. Where he once stood out for his athletic
prowess, he now was seen by some local townsfolk as a major threat
to the well-being of the community. Bill was a friendly guy who had
earned a reputation for liking to party. Having once said that his "drug
problem" began after his father died in the summer of 1968, it is more
likely that he began using drugs before he graduated from high school.
He generally was seen as a pretty mellow guy, but before long it was
apparent that he was getting some chemical help to tame the fears
and anxieties that had dominated his adolescent years. Although many

of the town's youth by that time had been introduced to marijuana, it was still viewed by local law enforcement as the "killer weed," largely responsible for the downfall of the nation's youth. With a good-paying factory job to ensure a steady supply of dope to smoke and a refrigerator filled with beer, Bill probably could have lived a contented, albeit mind-altered, life for a long time without the need for any change.

If Bill Fredericks had a nickel for every time that he showed bad judgment, he might have been well on his way to becoming rich. For Black men to think that they can get away with doing what white guys do is not just foolhardy but dangerous. Not only had Bill's drug usage become fairly widely known in the little town, but the die was cast when he was befriended by a young white high school guy who had already had his own run-ins with the law. Bobby, a brash motorcycle-riding hippie-type who looked like a character out of the movie *Easy Rider*, purportedly had been promised a deal to avoid prosecution if he would work as a "narc" to keep the police informed about drug activity in town. Bill would soon become a primary target. Already suspected of buying and reselling drugs brought into the area by college students at Kenyon, Bill also was openly dating a white girl whose family reportedly swore that they would put an end to the relationship . . . by any means necessary. This relationship, perhaps even more than his involvement in the area's marijuana trade, put him on local law enforcement's list as "public enemy number one."

In late summer of 1968, Bill had agreed to meet Bobby for a quick sale. How or why they picked the public square, almost in direct view of City Hall and the adjoining police department, wasn't clear. It only made sense if someone wanted to make it easy to observe the transaction. With his customary wide smile and gentle demeanor, Bill handed his eager, young customer a clear baggie containing a small quantity of marijuana in exchange for a crumpled five-dollar bill that Bobby had pushed deep into his jean's left-front pocket along with his keys. In the time it took Bill to push in his cigarette lighter and touch the hot end to his Marlboro, plainclothes police officers swiftly approached his maroon Buick convertible and pulled him roughly out of the car while ordering the several other guys who had crammed into his ride out as well. As they curtly announced that he was under arrest, the smile that once seemed permanently affixed to his face faded. Some would say that it would likely never in his lifetime reappear.

The headline in the newspaper reported that the "accused drug dealer faces 20 years to life." Even though the amount of marijuana sold was barely more than two grams, the charges included multiple counts of possession, possession for sale, and conspiracy to traffic in marijuana because Bill, unable to come up with more at the time of the police-arranged transaction, apologized and promised to bring Bobby more in a couple of days. Bill's distraught mother, Ina Mae, put her house up for bail to ensure her son's appearance for trial even though his skipping out on bond would mean that she would lose her home. While she managed to scrape together enough money to hire a Black lawyer from Mansfield, she probably had to ask her employer for an advance or loan. As the first African American attorney to set foot in a Knox County courthouse, Wilbur Flippen quickly learned how outsiders were regarded. And he was more than just an outsider. Not only was he a Black attorney treading where none had been before, he was representing a Black defendant that some badly wanted to see gone for good.

Although an experienced criminal defense attorney, Mr. Flippen underestimated just how much the prosecutor was determined to send Bill Fredericks away for a long time. Flippen challenged the excessive charges against his client and claimed that police misconduct had led to entrapment. He objected strenuously when it was mentioned at trial in front of the jury that Bill was dating a local girl whose family name was relatively well known. Knowing that it would evoke the ire of the jurors to hear that a Black drug user sold marijuana to local teenagers and dated white girls, the trial was as much spectacle as anything. With the testimony of their youthful informant and the statements of the officers who witnessed the exchange and made the arrest, the trial didn't last long.

In his closing arguments, the prosecutor asked the jury to send Bill and "those like him" a message. The message seemed to have less to do with marijuana usage that continued unabated throughout the community than it did with who the persons were who had the nerve to challenge the norms of the community. When he was arrested, Bill was in possession of a vial that contained one-tenth of a gram of hashish. Ultimately, he was convicted of possession for sale and dispensing of a narcotic drug, marijuana, and sentenced to a minimum of ten and up to twenty years' imprisonment in the state's medium-security prison at Mansfield. The lesson was driven home even further a short while later when a white Kenyon senior charged with the sale of LSD, a crime considered under Ohio law to be a more serious drug offense, saw his drug trafficking charges inexplicably reduced to mere possession. Allowed to finish his studies and graduate with his college class, Frank served less than two years at the honors farm at Grafton minimum security prison in northern Ohio, relatively close to his parents and hometown of Cleveland. He eventually attended law school and upon graduation was admitted to the bar after it was determined during the Supreme Court's routine "fitness to practice" check that he had the necessary good character to practice law in the state. Bill served nearly seven years in prison before being released . . . released from prison but not the ghosts that haunted him. Before long, he was arrested and charged with another drug offense, spending time once more in another prison. Even when not living behind bars, he remained captive to the poor decisions that plagued him his entire life.

CHAPTER 23

CONSEQUENCES OF RACISM

People can put a lot of pressure on themselves if they think that they must live their lives mistake free. It is even worse if you were raised by someone who, although well meaning, modeled for me what it was like to be afraid to fail and disappoint. Hell, my mother was pretty much afraid of the world. That leaves very little margin for error, whether it be in one's work or relationships. While it can at times provide impetus for doing one's job well, perhaps even excelling in one's career, there isn't much gratification if it stems from one's fears and insecurities. It's strange how I grew up being encouraged by a mother who insisted that her children could do anything that they put their minds to; yet, I rarely believed that I was smart enough, skilled enough, or deserving enough to "do good." It wasn't that I thought that I was incapable of accomplishing some of my goals, but I doubted that those accomplishments would be "enough." I later began to realize that many of these insecurities stemmed directly from the debilitating effects of persistent racism and racist ideologies.

Racism, consciously and subconsciously, impacts the emotional well-being of Black children. The effects are both detrimental and indelible; for me, they have been and will likely forever be with me for my entire life. Even if not said directly to me by the elders in my family, I just seemed to "know" that less would be expected of me over the course of my life because of the color of my skin. The old adage that "if you're Black, you need to be twice as good" was not lost on me. Not only did I set out to do most, if not all, of the things I attempted well, I was determined to "prove them wrong." In all likelihood, I was mostly afraid that my failures would confirm what they had believed all along. So, I tended to play it safe most of the time. I wasn't a risk taker and rarely attempted things at which I wasn't sure that I had a good chance to succeed.

Being told that parents of white schoolmates didn't want their daughters to even talk to me on the telephone sent the message that I wasn't good enough. These were constant reminders of the old adage that Black children come to know very early in their lives that "If you're Black, get back. If you're brown, stick around. If you're white, you're alright." I wasn't knowledgeable or wise enough at the time to appreciate how the legacy of racism against a backdrop of a pervasive and irrational fear that white people had of Black male sexuality would affect my life. So, by my teenage years I was struggling to prove myself worthy. And not just to be accepted by the families of the objects of some silly schoolboy crushes. I wanted to be seen as both capable and deserving, even when a high school guidance counselor tried to dissuade me from applying to one of the colleges on my modest list that was comprised of only two schools. He thought that I should set my sights lower. While I didn't know what the Ivy League was or represented to those more sophisticated about academia than I was, it was apparent when I informed him that I planned to apply to a school in Providence, Rhode Island, that he believed that I wasn't good enough. Fortunately, I didn't internalize that and end up feeling that I shouldn't aspire to go to college at all. Not long after, he was bragging to his colleagues that he helped get me into Brown University. The message that I received, once again, was that it was a fluke or mistake for my being admitted to one of the top colleges in the country, perhaps the only student in my class to be accepted to an Ivy. I shouldn't have been surprised that he didn't even ask me why I chose not to attend that prestigious university but opted, instead, to stay in Ohio to go to college in Cleveland. Looking back, I wonder how the poetry I began to write around that time in high school about racial conflict was influenced by my encounters while growing up in that small town surrounded by people like that.

CHAPTER 24

OFF TO THE BIG CITY

Going to college in a major city with a large African American population was both an eye-opening and soul-stirring experience. Although Cleveland had been in the news because of the recent racial unrest, I knew very little about it other than it was filled with poor Black people like my great-aunt Leona. As a very young child, I had gone with my mother to take my grandmother to visit her younger sister, Leona, on the east side of the city. While the sights of Black folks on porches and stoops everywhere was new and exciting in itself, it was accompanied by my mother's call for us to roll up our windows and make sure that the doors were locked. We certainly knew rural poverty, firsthand in fact, but being poor in the city, if for no reason other than its density, was something altogether different. It seemed to make her uneasy in ways that I had not seen in her before. These were reactions that I later came to associate with white people driving through Black communities. I didn't realize how much she, a mixed-race woman, must have felt like an outsider in Black America in addition to being the protective mother who constantly strove to keep her children safe. It saddens me to think how she and other Black people have internalized these negative perceptions of ourselves.

For Black youth of the 1960s and 1970s, college could be the time of cultural discovery and racial bonding. Even those not academically pre-

FIGURE 24.1. Ric managed to perfect a veneer in college that could
be read by outsiders, both Black and white, as intimidating and
unapproachable, just the opposite of who and what he really was.

pared or financially capable of attending college looked to the nation's
campuses for leaders who helped to shape the resistance strategies and
articulate the goals of "the movement." This was true for many who
lived in the rural towns and hamlets as well, although all the while fearful that the movement just might pass them by. Some found their connections to "real" Black culture vicariously when local colleges brought
national civil rights leaders to campus or held rallies and marches. You
didn't have to go to college to want to hear and believe that, as recited
by the young Rev. Jesse Jackson, "I AM Somebody." You didn't need
to take a college history class or a course in African American studies to understand that your station in life was due largely to the legacy
of slavery in American society. This was true even if you couldn't trace

your ancestral lineage to a specific plantation where your kinfolk were once held in bondage nor could you identify the nation or the people on the African continent from which you came.

Going to college in Cleveland frequently left me frustrated and confused. I immediately volunteered with social service agencies in the predominantly Black inner-city and took my first classes while a freshman in African American studies, that were taught by the only Black professor that I had in my entire four years of college. Early in my first year when I often was being recruited to live in the university's all-Black dormitory, I was referred to by members of the Black Student Union as a "pretty right-on brother, except . . ." In addition to not "sounding Black," I had a white girlfriend. Yes, she and I tried to transplant an immature relationship that began in a rural predominantly white high school to an urban university setting. The results weren't great. From one of the first (and few) times that we walked across campus together and I heard the admonition "that ain't good for ya, brother" come from a group of Black male students all dressed in military fatigues to our occasionally going over to see a movie at Strosaker Auditorium, I was conflicted. I wanted the Black students to see that I was every bit as committed to civil rights as they were, but I guess it was true that there was no such thing as color-blindness. It wasn't just that I "talked white" and had a white girlfriend, I was "country," hailing from rural environs as unfamiliar to them as if I had come from the moon.

Sadly, "Blackness" was as much performative as anything; if you came from a small town, you often didn't speak the same way, walk the same way, or navigate your environment as many of the urban Black students did or were accustomed to seeing. Frankly, you stood out and were as "different" to them as you were back home in the predominantly white community from which you came. And there was nothing more laughable to city Black folks than rural folks trying to act cool and sophisticated. I can't help but chuckle when I recall the efforts of the guys from my town to look like the Black guys in Columbus. My brother, cousin Bill, and a few of the other guys would drive the hour to Lee's Menswear on Mt. Vernon Avenue in the heart of Columbus' inner city to purchase their flashy, if not garish, walking suits. Decked out in a lime-green suit with bell bottom trousers accented by a black kick pleat and topped by a matching double-breasted jacket with large black buttons, Gregg just knew that he was looking "fly" even if at that time he hadn't heard that word before. But performing an acceptable Black style would require more than a change of clothes. Even to this day, I can detect a slight change in the cadence of our speech when members of my family are around just Black folks. Even when barely perceptible to some, I can almost feel the words roll from my mouth with an affectation, an attitude if you will. Then, I begin to feel embarrassed when I think that doing that probably is no less contrived as white folks attempting to speak with what they imagine to be authentic Negro dialect. If it wasn't so annoying, it would be funny to hear them trying to sound "Blacker" than I do.

Going to school in Cleveland was a challenge for me. What was becoming apparent was that I was feeling alienated from both white and Black students on Case's campus. I didn't expect much from the white students, most of whom hadn't had Black friends before or during college. They often were as leery or distrusting of me as they were of all other Black people. It didn't matter that I have lived and gone to school with folks who looked like them my entire life. Fortunately, I didn't feel a need to bond with them since I was working to extract myself from my high school days anyway. I had not anticipated that it would be so hard to find common ground with Black students from the urban areas. They could be as judgmental and disapproving as the white students were. I later discovered that this wasn't my experience alone; my older siblings felt the pressures as well. Other Black students from small towns have relayed similar experiences about their struggles to fit in.

By the time that I went to college, the first wave of the formal Black Power movement was waning. Many colleges and universities had given in to the demands of their Black students to open cultural houses and create Black dormitories or living spaces. Case Western Reserve University, although a sizeable university of approximately eight thousand students among its several colleges, graduate programs, and professional schools, had relatively few African American students on its large campus. There were so few of us that it wasn't unusual to be stopped by campus police while walking at night from the gym or Allen Library and asked to show some identification. The university was essentially plopped down on the edge of a predominantly Black community on the east side of Cleveland, what some referred to as an oasis in the middle of a Black desert. In other words, it was the classic example of wealthy institutions buying up property in a segregated and blighted neighborhood. The primary plan called for razing what had been most of the moderate and low-income housing stock that would eventually drive poor Black people away from the periphery of campus. CWRU and other renowned cultural institutions like the internationally famous Cleveland Museum of Art and Cleveland Symphony Orchestra were the jewels of University Circle, and their luster had to be preserved at all cost. These institutions worked hard to safeguard their impressive treasures, inside and out, including their walking spaces, from unwelcome trespassers who just happened to look like me.

As had been the practice at many private colleges, all of the Black students at Case back then were automatically considered members of the Black Student Union. During my first year of college, I regularly attended meetings held in the lounge of the Black dorm, Sherman House. The typical grievances about the college and society at large were aired at many of the meetings. The main priority, however, seemed to be organizing the social lives of the Black students. Committees were formed to organize the parties, events, and the yearly formal. Unlike most of my male (and many female) counterparts, I hadn't come to college to "get my groove on"; thus, I didn't volunteer for any committees. By then, it was pretty clear to me that they weren't going to be receptive to my bringing my white girlfriend to the events, even if I had the courage and self-confidence to do so. And, the "sisters" were pretty hard on the couple of Black guys who were known or even suspected to be messing around with white girls. I assumed that those who didn't know that my girlfriend was white must have concluded that I might have been gay since I didn't respond in typical fashion to their attempts to hit on me. I recall one young woman who lived in the dorm inviting me up to her room after a meeting. After some small

talk, she shook her head and said, "Humph, man, you are really different . . . it ain't like I'm not offering you some . . . you just don't seem
the least bit interested."

My social life, if you want to call it that, was pretty sad. When I
wasn't in class or studying, I spent a lot of time playing basketball. It
was my primary outlet. Other than a friendship that I struck up with a
guy who was from a small town, the time that I wasn't alone was time
spent holed up with my girlfriend in my dorm or her apartment. She
had the misfortune of going off to college with a high school boyfriend; worse yet, it was a boyfriend who was struggling to figure out
who he was and was limited by his fears and insecurities. It was no surprise that the one close friendship that I formed was with a guy that I
later learned I had met while we were in high school. He, too, was one
of only a handful of students of color in his high school, a high school
that just happened to be across town from my own and within walking
distance of the house in which I had grown up. What were the chances
that I would meet and become close friends with a mixed-race guy
who went to high school in Mt. Vernon? John, who grew up in Oberlin, Ohio, was the son of an African American mother and Mexican
immigrant father. Raised as a Seventh Day Adventist, he attended high
school at the Mt. Vernon Academy, the small church-based school on
the edge of my hometown. We discovered shortly after meeting that
we had played basketball against one another when our high school
teams scrimmaged in the preseason.

Our meeting at college happened as a direct consequence of our
respective shyness and defense mechanisms. It was my habit to go to
the college's dining hall as soon as it opened for dinner to avoid arriving after the tables were already filled. The stress of choosing where to
sit or having to join a table of strangers was intimidating for me. So, I
always managed to get to the dining hall in time to find an empty table
and sit at the end, hanging my jacket on the back of the chair next to
me and spreading out my things to prevent anyone from encroaching
upon my personal space.

On a day when the dining hall seemed to fill quickly, in walked this
handsome young man with a tray in hand looking for a place to sit. My

table, as was customary, was empty after I had constructed my usual barriers. He walked over and took a seat at the other end. He pulled off his jacket and hung it on the back of the seat next to him, as if to reinforce the blockade that I had already set up. Soon thereafter, I looked up after he asked me to pass down the salt and pepper shakers. It was then that I noticed his letterman's jacket. Prominently placed on the varsity letter sewn to the front was "Mt. Vernon Academy." I surprised even myself when I asked him where his school was. He responded that it was in a small town a couple of hours away that I had probably never heard of. Not only had I heard of it, I lived there, literally within a couple miles of his high school.

Thus, began a friendship that literally got me through college. To the extent that I let him, and he let me, we really got each other. He was religious, and I was moving away from my religious roots. I was concerned about issues of race and justice; he was into science and aiming for medical school. Since that time, I realized that we really didn't have all that much in common, except we both grew up as "one of the only" in our respective schools and communities, playing sports as a way to fit in, and because we were good at them. Academic achievers, successful athletes, and social introverts, we thought we knew how the other felt a lot of the time. More importantly, we felt that we could trust each other . . . and did. He was one of the few who routinely saw through the mask. He knew that the seemingly imposing veneer, the scowl, and impenetrable dark glasses were all part of an act. If I looked unapproachable, then perhaps no one would mess with me. Life took us in different directions, following different paths; yet, strangely enough when we managed to get in contact, infrequently as it was and usually after the passage of several years, it was almost as if we had been talking with one another regularly for much of our lives. I felt compelled some years ago to write to him after I received tenure to let him know how important he was to me when we were growing up. I've seen John maybe five times over nearly forty-five years since our college days. To this day, I feel a special fondness for him and think about him from time to time. When next we meet, maybe he'll see that I've grown since those days.

THANK YOU
'TIL YOU'RE BETTER PAID

To the casual observer, it may seem as though Black folks from rural America generally, and my family in particular, have traveled a long way from those days when life's opportunities were strictly defined by the demarcation known as the "color line." Yet, it is important that we not forget how circumscribed our lives have been for generations. Baseball major leaguer Yogi Berra's famous quip "It gets late early out there" may well have applied to his home state of Missouri's numerous sundown towns and those that sprang up in Ohio. It easily could have been borrowed from Black folks who knew firsthand its unmistakable meaning in rural parts of the Midwest. Over time, the nation has come to see that the not-so-uncommon admonition that we were not welcome in certain communities was not limited just to spaces where the air was fresh and the sky remarkably blue. At the same time, those of us who have lived in small-town Ohio are faced with constant reminders that there will be no blending in or true sense of belonging in our rural communities as long as race is the most defining factor in American society and we remain oddities at best or, at worst, seen as dangerous, frightening spectacles in need of special control in our own hometowns.

Hard work and good fortune have resulted in many rewards over my lifetime. Professionally, I have held challenging and rewarding positions throughout my career. I've been one of the lucky ones; I have never had to take a job that I didn't want or believe would enable me to do things that ultimately would make a difference. That young man who left home at seventeen hoping to one day get a job as a social worker so he could help make the world a better place has had the good fortune of working in positions where he genuinely felt that what he was doing really did make a difference. I have never had to deviate or settle for employment that was inconsistent with that goal, and I've never been unemployed. Those opportunities came to me despite the personal insecurities and cultural challenges that could have easily derailed me during this journey. Admittedly, I still have to work to allow myself to acknowledge when a job has been done well or maybe even just good enough. In the end, this would seem to suggest a great deal of success. Yet, looking more deeply, one begins to see the fissures that reveal what a struggle it has been to free myself from the constraints of racism and its lasting effects in an environment where so few people can see it or are willing to acknowledge it.

While I'm often told that I don't accept compliments well, I've come to realize that it isn't just because I'm shy or reserved, having been somewhat introverted for most of my life. When young people feel as though they are doubted from the beginning, I know that the impact upon self-confidence can last for an entire lifetime. I think when you are constantly saddled with feelings of "imposter syndrome," it is hard to accept praise. When you grew up in a family with modest means, you can't help but wonder why you were the one so fortunate to escape the usual predictions for a Black male raised in low-income, working-class America. I saw relatives have run-ins with the law, even when it was mostly their fault, and end up serving unusually harsh prison sentences for behaviors that were common among white youth in my town that often went unpunished. Experiences like that tend to make you remain on guard so as not to have encounters that can lead to serious trouble . . . or worse, death.

When I think about how over the course of my life I've felt compelled to conduct myself, the word *cautious* doesn't quite get it. I suppose that it is no coincidence that I've never even as much as received a speeding ticket after more than fifty years of driving. Or that I never purchased a vehicle with heavily tinted window glass that might cause a police officer to be overly nervous about approaching my car. Or that I keep my car registration in plain sight under the visor so that I never have to reach into the glove compartment to get the papers. Or that I would never remove my hands from the steering wheel if pulled over by police or place them in my pockets while in a store. And, while many, if not most, of my peers were experimenting with soft drugs and alcohol growing up, I was too fearful of the consequences to join in. It wasn't because I wasn't curious or tempted nor that I felt morally superior to anyone. I just knew that if I screwed up in my small town, I would come to regret it in ways disproportionate to the seriousness of the behavior. Maybe, just maybe, I also felt that I owed it to my grandparents and my parents to make the most of the opportunities that I had, and so many others never got. My mother often said to me, "You know your dad would have been so proud." I was afraid to "pay the price," and I definitely didn't want to bring shame to them.

Today's overused phrase "pay it forward" always had meaning to me, even as a young person, as corny as that might seem. When so many Americans of all races are struggling to make it, sometimes simply to just survive, I've come to understand much better why I feel that I have an obligation to look beyond myself in my quest to know my purpose. My modest successes have become both the pride of my family and the victories of a people. And my disappointments are never borne alone, just as I was taught that my failures of character reflected negatively on all people who look like me. "Don't you mess up and live down to their expectations, boy."

Looking back across the generations, I'm struck by how much grit and determination have played a role in the fortunes of this family. While this story is the story of so many who have lived the lives of "small-town cullud folks," it is also the American story of families that migrated to and throughout this country. It is a story of hard luck and good fortune, while at the same time being a story of heartache and redemption. It is a story of plain, ordinary people who managed to persevere under circumstances when many others did not. Most of all, it is a story of a family where love was the common denominator. Regardless of the mistakes and missteps over time, of which there were many, the descendants continued to carry on, all the while revering the matriarch, Bertha Ruthanna Edwards Fisher Hammonds, whose soul and spirit reminded us all to put others first before ourselves. Thanks a million, Bertha, 'til you're better paid.

FIGURE 25.1. Oneida with her five children (L to R):
Ric, Karen, Oneida, Debra, Lori, and Gregg.

AUTHOR'S NOTE

This project began as a modest attempt to jot down some family memories for my siblings as well as our children. Aging is often the impetus for documenting lineage and attaching names to faces in faded photographs. While it has become increasingly more common for families to embark upon genealogical expeditions that often result in detailed charts, my wish was to share some of the inspiring stories that gave life to these relationships. While lists and fancy "family trees" may be interesting to a handful of us for whom the branches reveal connections, they are incapable of stirring the soul the way that a "good telling" through the oral traditions practiced over generations can do. I had imagined, and continue to hope, that this book would be only the beginning of a collection of narratives and events less well known. Perhaps others will take up the mantle and move this project further. These are the true treasures with which we have been gifted by our ancestors. The greatest family legacies are those that can reside eternally in the hearts of its members.

The writing began in earnest when the nation found itself confronted by the coronavirus pandemic. My ninety-two-year-old mother was residing in an area nursing home. Consistent with many of the experiences conveyed in these writings, she spent her final years, not unlike much of the rest of her life, as the only person of color in her surroundings. Initially, in a senior assisted-living apartment complex populated by a handful of persons with whom she had common acquaintances going back as far as high school, she wore her familiar smile to match her pleasant personality that had worked for decades to ease her acceptance in this all-white space.

Later, when she found herself unceremoniously moved into a nursing home, again with only white faces, there was substantially less social interaction. The rather obvious stares from a few of the other residents, especially when her brown-skinned family visited, may have been less distressing for her by that time since she may not have had the cognitive ability to understand that once again she was a spectacle. During the several months that none of us were able to visit her, she was never in the company of anyone who shared her cultural experiences or a skin tone that announced a kinship at any level regardless of how remote.

I had almost forgotten that for older Black folks in rural America there can be more than one type of isolation and that it didn't have to stem from the lack of visitors or other social interaction. While all of the residents of that nursing home likely suffered from the absence of contact with loved ones, particularly during the pandemic, my mother may have felt even more isolated due to the fact that no one in the physical space that she occupied, staff or resident, looked like her. Of course, she never voiced any distress about her circumstances, either because she didn't know how or as a result of her illness wasn't able to do so. While I could imagine some sense of discomfort, perhaps a lot like that experienced during most of her life where she was often "the only one," I couldn't help but wonder if, somehow, she was resigned to this thing that was familiar to her and with which she had learned to cope for so long. To this day, I am still uncertain as to just how "alone" she felt during those years.

Life has a way of bringing a sense of urgency to our family relationships and aspirations. As I furiously researched to discover more documents and to record statements confirming the facts underlying these stories, I knew that I was in a race against time. With a renewed sense of purpose, I combed through the photo albums and reached out to the handful of living relatives who could fill in some of the blanks. While many writing projects often begin with no end date in mind, I feared that one would be imposed upon me whether I had planned or intended for there to be one or not. Something inside of me doubted that I would have the emotional strength to continue this project if, perhaps I should say when, my mother would leave this world. So, I was intent on finishing it as quickly as I could and made good progress by setting aside a couple of hours each morning.

I am extremely grateful to my siblings—Gregg Sheffield, Karen Sheffield, Anika Sheffield Harris, and Lori Lawson Turner—for allowing me to read them chapters of my manuscript. I did it less to confirm the accuracy of my accounts than to share with them the joy of discovery of the extraordinary stories of love and perseverance. It also provided special moments of recollections and remembrances during the many hours of readings and conversation. With our mother in hospice care and the end nearing, these weekly, sometimes twice weekly, virtual gatherings provided some degree of solace as well as joy. The time we came together was a gift to me and, I hope, to them as well. I managed to finish the manuscript (as if anyone truly finishes any writing) by the end of September. I feel especially grateful and blessed that I was able to read portions of this book to Maurice Sheffield, my still adventurous uncle at age ninety-four, and his sister, Lula Sheffield Williams, the family matriarch who was making plans to celebrate her one-hundredth birthday at the time.

Within a couple of weeks of my completing the conclusion to this book, our mother, "Miss Oneida" as they called her at the nursing home, passed away. Two days before her passing, I sat at her bedside with the printed manuscript splayed across my lap. Taking her tiny, frail hand into mine, I told her that I loved her with all of my heart—"except for the parts reserved for Ellen and my kids," a running joke that we had shared for years. I thanked her for being a caring and wonderful mother to me. Then, I told her that I had begun to write some things down so that I could share them with our family and preserve those thoughts for when my own memories began to fade. In my customary way of teasing her, I told her that I had to write things down like she had done for so many years because I, too, was fast approaching the time when I wouldn't remember the stories that needed to be told and that otherwise would likely be lost forever.

With my voice breaking on occasion, I read a couple of chapters to her that recalled her mother's life. Pausing from time to time to scan her face for any sign of recognition of the names that spilled out, especially her mother Bertha's name or even her own, I intently watched as her closed eyelids quivered and danced. I prayed that the vivid recollections might move her to smile someplace deep within her, even if not outwardly. As I read to her, I remembered on one particular occasion, prior to her losing her ability to speak, that she seemed to know that her time was coming. She looked into my face and said, "My mother's waiting for me. She's ready for me to join her." When I returned the next day, I was met at the nurse's station, where they intercepted me before I could return to my mother's room. Before I could go in they would need some time "to prepare her," they told me. While I knew instantly what they meant, the staff didn't fully understand me when I replied that she had already been prepared . . . by her mother. Her daily prayers answered, they would be together once more at last. And, despite my own grief, I am happy that they are finally reunited.

ACKNOWLEDGMENTS

This book is a direct result of the encouragement of many. That encouragement came from those, like my siblings, who were deeply invested in the stories that I would ultimately tell and share with our whole family. Their interest and delight confirmed that this indeed would be the gift to my family that I was hoping to give. I was encouraged by the first readers of portions of the manuscript. I am particularly grateful to Mary Ann McNair at StoryCenter, who was among the first to read portions as they unfolded. Mary Ann convinced me that the narratives would have value to many beyond those named in them and that the way in which they were told could touch others as well.

While she didn't know it, author and writing instructor Nancy Zafris was an encouraging presence for me in producing this work. Even before I found the courage to take a Kenyon Review Writer's Workshop on nonfiction writing, Nancy read an essay that I wrote about Marian Anderson and attended a talk that I had given on my research about the great singer. The screenplay that Nancy subsequently produced based upon my research and essay gave me confidence that I was learning to become an effective storyteller. So, I feel compelled to acknowledge the effect that her encouragement had upon this manuscript and my subsequent writing.

As has been the case for many of my professional endeavors over the past thirty years, Howard Sacks has been both mentor and friend. I turned to him when I needed advice and counsel. Often, I went to him when I just needed some reassurance that I wasn't getting caught up in the emotion of writing about things so personal and that I had closely guarded for most of my life. It was Howard who ultimately encouraged me to pursue the publication of this book. I trust his judgment, so his feedback played a large part in this project taking this direction and ultimately seeing the light of day.

Sometimes, it seems like a cliché when authors thank their children. For me, though, I know that I am inspired every day by my daughter, Camille, and sons, Clark and Cuy. I know that their presence in my life has given it meaning that transcends all space and time, even when we are thousands of miles apart and began long before their first breaths. It is said that a person never dies so long as they are remembered with love in the hearts of others. That is the true gift of family and largely why this book exists. If we are blessed, it may help to keep those family loved ones alive for generations to come. In the end, though, I am most grateful to my wife, Ellen, for her patience and support for this and all of the projects that I've undertaken in what must seem to be an endless journey exploring the complex issues of identity and rural roots for those of us who often haven't felt welcome or that we belonged. For nearly the entirety of my life, she is and has been my inspiration and my best friend.

TIMELINE

Note: Persons' racial classifications often changed between census years or document sources (e.g., from mulatto to colored, colored to Black, Black to Negro, colored to white or vice versa); sometimes race was misidentified or left blank altogether. For purposes of this timeline, two or more classifications will be listed when more than one classification appears in or on an official record; sometimes race will be inferred from documents that specify the race of a person's parents.

1818   Jane Eliza Clark (white) born in England, immigrated to the US.

1820   Mary Fraser Fisher (white) born in Ireland, immigrated to US, worked as servant at time she met Jim Fisher (Black) who she later married.

1824   Elisha Edwards Sr. (Black) born in Virginia.

1825   James Fisher (Black) born in Virginia.

1849   Ohio Legislature provides for mandatory schooling and the creation of separate schools for colored children where numbers exceed twenty.

1850   Katherine (Cherin) Sheffield (white) born in Horse Pasture, Henry County, Virginia.

1854   Charles Bell Smiley (Black) born in Louisville, Kentucky; birth record fails to show mother's name. "Father or owner" may be E. D. Hobbs. Smiley name has been said to come from William Smiley.

1855   Sarah Ellen Tucker (white) born to Gus Tucker (white) and Jane Eliza Clark Tucker (white) in Guernsey County, Ohio.

1856   Stephen A. Fisher (Black) born to Jim Fisher (Black) and Mary Parker Fisher (white, from Ireland); died 1935.

1858   Elisha (June) Edwards Jr. born to Elisha T. Edwards and Mary Ann Buckney Edwards in Barnesville, Belmont County, Ohio.

1861   Elisha Edwards Sr. enlists in the Union Army to fight with the colored troops in the Civil War, serving three years.

1862   Samuel Sheffield born to Katherine (listed as "Cherin" in some sources, race not designated) Sheffield and Hobart Sheffield (Black).

1863   George W. Edwards (Black), oldest brother of June Edwards, enlists in Union Army and is appointed to the rank of corporal. He was reduced in rank the following winter. He was captured at battle of Brice's Cross Roads in June of 1864. He was held captive in Andersonville and other confederate prisons. Mustered out in August 1865.

1865   13th Amendment to Constitutions strikes down slavery in the US.

1868   14th Amendment to Constitution establishes so-called Equal Protection and citizenship for all persons born in the country.

1870   15th Amendment to Constitution is passed and intended to protect against denying Black men the vote on account of race.

         Ben Snowden (Black) attempts to vote in Knox County and is turned away, files lawsuit against election judges but loses case six years later.

1871   Fisk Jubilee Singers, during their first national tour, perform a concert in Mt. Vernon, Ohio, at the First Congregational Church.

1873   Wayman Chapel AME Church founded in Mt. Vernon, Ohio, becoming the first Black congregation in Knox County, Ohio.

1877   Jennie Nancy Johnson born to John Henry Johnson (white) and Catherine Johnson (white) in Belmont County, Ohio.

1878   Leon ("Lon") Guthrie Hammonds (colored, Black) born in Chillicothe, Ross County, Ohio.

1880   The US Census reports 319 Black residents in Knox County, Ohio.

1883   Lawsuit filed by Black youth in Mt. Vernon under Ohio's newly enacted Civil Rights Law for denial of access to local skating rink. Case settled.

1884   Stephen Fisher marries Sarah Ellen Tucker.

1886   Matilda Ann (Tillie Mae) Smiley (colored) born to Charles Smiley (Black) and Eliza Harvey Smiley (mulatto born into slavery; "owned" by Dr. Frazee) in Louisville, Kentucky.

1895   Samuel Walton Sheffield born to Samuel Sheffield and Lula ("Loula") Sheffield in Henry County, Virginia.

1896   Elisha June Edwards (colored, Black) and Jennie Nancy Johnson (white), born in Boston, Massachusetts, marry in Belmont County, Ohio.

1899   Bertha Ruthanna Edwards (colored/mulatto) born to June Edwards (Black) and Jennie Nancy Johnson (white) in Barnesville, Belmont County, Ohio.

1900   Lon Hammonds migrates north from Chillicothe, Ross County, Ohio, to Mt. Vernon, Knox County, Ohio.

        The census records show 632 Black persons in Belmont County; 104 in Knox County; and 29 in Coshocton County.

1902   Arthur Fisher (colored, mulatto) born to Stephen Fisher (Black, mulatto) and Sarah Ellen Tucker Fisher (white, Irish) in Guernsey County, Ohio.

1903   Herman Edwards (colored, mulatto) born to June Edwards (colored, Black) and Jennie Nancy Johnson (white) in Barnesville, Belmont County, Ohio.

1904   Baptist Mission is formed in Mt. Vernon by Black migrants from Circleville, Ohio, who came to work at the C&G Cooper Company; Elder Bryant presides.

1905   George Copeland (Black) of Mt. Vernon accused of rape and murder of a white woman, Miranda Bricker; charges later dropped after barely averting a lynching.

1910   The census records show 1,782 Black persons in Belmont County; 323 in Knox County; and 97 in Coshocton County.

1912   Eva Juanita Felton Edwards born (parents unknown) and then adopted by Emanuel and Dora Felton in Coshocton, Ohio.

1914   Mt. Calvary Baptist Church built in Mt. Vernon, becoming the second Black church to be founded in the community.

1916   Lon Hammonds begins to work at Essex Glass Company in Mt. Vernon, Knox County, Ohio.

1917   Matilda Smiley Graham (colored, Black) moves with her husband, John Graham (Black), and family to Coshocton, Ohio.

        East St. Louis, Illinois, riots where hundreds of Black residents were killed by white mobs and thousands left homeless; violence was said to have been precipitated by labor strife and competition for jobs brought about by migration of Blacks from the south.

1918   Lon Hammonds registers for the draft in Knox County, Ohio, at the age of forty; World War I ended within two months, never called for active duty.

        Ben Carter becomes the first Black soldier from Mt. Vernon to be killed during World War I; one of those who avoided contracting Spanish flu.

1919   John Graham dies, leaving his widow, Matilda, and five children.

1920   Sam Sheffield Sr. (colored, Black) marries the recently widowed Tillie Mae Graham.

        Ku Klux Klan acquires the Hiawatha Lake Park in Mt. Vernon; property later acquired by Knox County and becomes the county fairgrounds.

        US Census reports show that there are 420 Black residents in Knox County, Ohio, representing nearly 4% of Mt. Vernon's population; 2,029 in Belmont County; and 144 in Coshocton County.

1921   Lula Estelle Sheffield (colored, Black) born in Coshocton, Ohio, to Sam Sheffield Sr. and Matilda Smiley Graham Sheffield.

        Tulsa, Oklahoma, race massacre occurs when white mobs, fueled by rumors of an assault by a Black teenager on a white female elevator operator, indiscriminately attack Black residents, killing at least three dozen Black residents and burning much of the business district in the Greenwood section of the city known as Black Wall Street to the ground.

1922 Sam Sheffield Jr. (colored, Black) born to Sam Sheffield Sr. and Matilda (Tillie) Mae Smiley Graham Sheffield in Mayberry, West Virginia.

1923 Ina Mae Fisher born to Bertha Edwards Fisher and Arthur Fisher in Belmont County.

1924 Mary Jane Fisher (colored) born in Barnesville to Bertha Edwards Fisher and Arthur Fisher.

1928 Oneida Fisher (colored, Black) born in Coshocton, Coshocton County, Ohio, to Bertha Edwards Fisher (colored, mulatto) and Art Fisher (colored, mulatto).

1929 US economy sinks, starting era called the Great Depression.

1930 US Census reports show that there are 392 Black residents in Knox County, Ohio; 2,699 in Belmont County; and 225 in Coshocton County.

1931 Herman Edwards jailed in Coshocton, Ohio, for public intoxication.

Nine Black teenagers wrongly convicted of raping two white women and sentenced to die in infamous case in Scottsboro, Alabama.

1932 US Supreme Court overturns Scottsboro convictions in *Powell v. Alabama,* holding boys did not have adequate legal representation; collectively, they spent more than 100 years in prison during the course of the several trials and appeals of the decisions.

1932 Herman Edwards (colored/mulatto) and Eva Felton Mueller (white), wife of Clarence Mueller, arrested for cohabitation. Eva was placed on probation, and Herman was ordered to leave town.

1933 Black youth organize entertainment to raise money to build tennis court at the home of Lon Hammonds.

Sarah Ellen Fisher dies in Cambridge, Ohio.

1936 Lon Hammonds divorces Ethel Simmons Reynolds (colored) in Knox County, Ohio.

1938 Arthur Fisher is killed when run over by truck driven by his brother-in-law Herman Edwards in Barnesville, Belmont County, Ohio.

Lon Hammonds and Bertha Fisher marry in Knox County, Ohio, four months after Art Fisher dies.

Elisha June Edwards, Bertha's father, dies on his farm in Belmont County, Ohio.

Betty Lou (Fisher) Thompson born to Mary Jane Fisher; Bertha Edwards Fisher's first grandchild.

1939   Ben Carter Post 349 of American Legion founded for Black veterans who generally weren't welcome as members of legion posts in Mt. Vernon; post named after first Black soldier killed in World War I.

1940   Sam Sheffield Jr. drops out of Coshocton High School and joins the federal Civilian Conservation Corps out of Zanesville, Ohio.

Sam Sheffield Jr. and five other Black youth in Coshocton, Ohio, are charged with rape and convicted of attempted rape of a white woman after guilty pleas are given under questionable circumstances; none sent to prison.

Sam Sheffield Jr. enlists in the U.S Army, stationed in Arizona, Mississippi, and Alaska. Serves in the Pacific Theatre during WWII.

Rev. Charles Bell Smiley, father of Tillie Mae Sheffield, dies at her home in Coshocton, Ohio. He was predeceased by his wife and eight of thirteen children.

US Census reports show that there are 361 Black residents in Knox County, Ohio; 2,415 in Belmont County; and 216 in Coshocton County.

1945   Sam Sheffield Jr. is honorably discharged from the Army with the rank of sergeant, thought to have contracted chronic illness while serving in Asian Pacific Theatre during WWII.

1946   Oneida Fisher graduates from Mt. Vernon High School and attends Mt. Vernon Business College.

1947   Oneida Fisher competes in the Miss Bronze Ohio pageant in Columbus, Ohio; among the more than 120 women in the pageant were ten other women from Mt. Vernon; Oneida Fisher finishes fourth.

Oneida Fisher takes job as legal secretary for Black lawyer, Stewart Calhoun, in Keystone, West Virginia.

Sam Sheffield Jr. and Oneida Fisher marry at the home of Lon and Bertha Hammonds in Mt. Vernon, Ohio.

1948   Bill King is born in Welch, West Virginia, raised by John and Ina Mae Fredericks in Mt. Vernon, subsequently adopted when he is in high school.

1949   Gregg Sheffield is the first child born to Oneida and Sam Sheffield Jr. in Mt. Vernon, Ohio.

1950   According to US Census, 414 Black people call Knox County, Ohio home, the second largest documented Black population.

Karen Sheffield is the second child born to Oneida and Sam Sheffield Jr. in Mt. Vernon, Ohio.

Decree passed by the Mt. Vernon YMCA that membership will be open to all regardless of race, creed, or color.

1953   Debra Sheffield is the third child born to Oneida and Sam Sheffield Jr. in Mt. Vernon, Ohio.

1954   Ricci Sheffield is the fourth child born to Oneida and Sam Sheffield Jr. in Mt. Vernon, Ohio; he is named after Sam's Italian American friend from the service whose family "Americanized" their last name by pronouncing it as if it were spelled Ricky.

US Supreme Court decides in *Brown v. Board of Education* case that racially segregated, separate schools are not equal and thus unconstitutional under the 14th amendment.

Jeffrey J. Jackson is born to Betty Lou (Fisher) Thompson and Floyd Jackson; he is Bertha Fisher Hammonds' first great-grandchild.

1955   Emmett Till is murdered and lynched in Mississippi after being accused of offending a white woman; disfigured body in casket shown in newspapers.

1956   Sam Sheffield Jr. begins treatment for spells at Veteran's Hospital in Cleveland, Ohio; goes in and out of hospital, possible diagnosis is MS.

1958   Sam Sheffield Jr. dies in Mt. Vernon as a result of self-inflicted gunshot wound to the head; death ruled a suicide by coroner.

1960   US Census reports show that there are 380 Black residents in Knox County, Ohio; 2,071 in Belmont County; and 356 in Coshocton County.

1963   Oneida Sheffield marries George F. Lawson of Columbus, Ohio.

Civil Rights activist Medgar Evers assassinated in Mississippi.

United States President John F. Kennedy assassinated in Dallas, Texas.

Lori Lynn Lawson born to Oneida and George Lawson on Christmas Day; she is Bertha Hammonds' last grandchild.

1964   Audrey Holt becomes first Black elementary school teacher in Knox County; Gilbert Newsome becomes first Black high school teacher.

Civil Rights activists James Chaney, Andrew Goodman, and Michael Schwerner found murdered in Mississippi.

1965   Voting Rights Act is passed by US Congress.

Malcolm X, Black nationalist and human rights activist, assassinated in New York City.

1967   Civil Rights Conference held at Kenyon College in neighboring Gambier.

Thurgood Marshall appointed to the United States Supreme Court, becoming the nation's first Black justice.

1968   Reverend Martin Luther King Jr. assassinated in Memphis, Tennessee.

Herman and Eva Edwards shot and killed by Pauline Porter, the mother of Norma Jean Edward's fiancé, Bill (white) in Barnesville, Ohio.

1969   Tillie Mae Sheffield dies at age eighty-two in Coshocton, Ohio.

Black Student Union is founded at Kenyon College in neighboring Gambier; first president is Roland Parson, who subsequently marries Mt. Vernon resident and Kenyon employee Karen Sheffield.

1970   Knox County Chapter of the NAACP is founded, boasting sixty-five members by end of first year; first president is Gene Fields of Mt. Vernon.

John Fredericks dies in Mt. Vernon.

Bill King Fredericks arrested and convicted of drug charges.

Tamara Vashti Parson born to Roland Parson and Karen Sheffield Parson; she is Oneida Sheffield Lawson's first grandchild.

US Census reports show that there are 345 Black residents in Knox County, Ohio; 1,804 in Belmont County; and 323 in Coshocton County.

1971   Charles Chancellor elected to Mt. Vernon Board of Education, first Black person elected to public office in Mt. Vernon.

Debra Sheffield becomes first Black girl chosen by student body as Forum Queen at Mt. Vernon High School.

1983   Bertha Ruthanna Edwards Hammonds dies in Mt. Vernon just a few days shy of her 84th birthday.

Stanley White dies in Mt. Vernon at age 64.

1987   Rev. Sam Sheffield Sr. dies in Henry County, Virginia. at the age of 92 years old.

Ina Mae Fisher Fredericks dies in Mt. Vernon at age 64.

1990   Cuyler Neil Sheffield born to Ellen Clark Sheffield and Ric Samuel Sheffield; he is Oneida Sheffield Lawson's youngest grandchild.

1993   Ku Klux Klan holds a rally approximately 30 miles away in Coshocton, Ohio.

1995   Mary Jane Fisher White dies in Mt. Vernon at the age of 71.

2000   George F. Lawson, Oneida's second husband and Lori Lynn Lawson's father, dies at 78 in Mt. Vernon.

2001   Mercedes (Mick) Reyes-Parson born to Tamara Parson and Miquel Estrada Reyes; Oneida Sheffield Lawson's first great-grandchild.

2008   Barack Obama, a mixed-raced Senator from Illinois, becomes the first African American to be elected president of the United States.

2012   Barack Obama re-elected to the office of the president of the United States.

2020   Oneida Fisher Sheffield Lawson dies at nursing home in Mt. Vernon.

BIBLIOGRAPHY

PRIMARY SOURCES

Coshocton High School yearbook "Room Six—Freshmen," 1937, Coshocton, Ohio

Interviews and interview transcripts with Oneida Sheffield Lawson, Lula Williams, Maurice Sheffield, Dian Hammonds Ryuse, Florine White, Rev. Harold Turner, James Payne, and Mary Jane White

National Archives; Civilian Conservation Corps records, https://www.archives.gov/research/guide-fed-records/groups/035.html

National Archives; United States Census records, https://www.archives.gov/research/genealogy/census

Ohio Department of Vital Statistics; various county birth, death, and marriage records

United States Department of Veteran affairs; military registration, assignment, and discharge records

SECONDARY SOURCES

"Attack on Girl Is Admitted by Four, Three Negroes Plead Not Guilty to Charge in Mayor's Court," *Coshocton Tribune* (Coshocton, Ohio), June 15, 1940, page 1.

"Barnesville Couple Are Double Murder Victims," *Barnesville Enterprise,*
    March 28, 1968, page 1.

"Beauties Promenade," *The Ohio State News,* July 26, 1947, page 1.

"Coshocton News," *Cleveland Call and Post,* September 28, 1940, page A4.

"Coroner to Rule in Sheffield Death," *Mount Vernon (Ohio) News,* March 3,
    1958, page 3.

"Costumes, Interesting Faces Abound on Streets of Mount Vernon; Plays
    Butler: Sam Sheffield plays the role of butler," *Mount Vernon (Ohio)
    News,* July 8, 1955, page 2.

"Court Sets Negroes Free on Probation," *Coshocton Tribune* (Coshocton,
    Ohio), September 20, 1940, page 3.

"Death of Former Coshocton Man Is Investigated," *Coshocton Tribune*
    (Coshocton, Ohio), March 2, 1958, page 1.

"Death of Former Resident Probed," *Coshocton Tribune* (Coshocton, Ohio),
    March 2, 1958, page 3.

"Ft. Huachuca [*sic*]," *Cleveland Call and Post,* May 10, 1941, page A19.

"'Miss Ohio' Contestants," *The Ohio State News,* June 14, 1947, page 1.

"Negroes Free on Probation, Held for Rape, They Are Allowed to Plead to
    Lesser Charge," *Coshocton Tribune* (Coshocton, Ohio), September 20,
    1940, page 1.

"Priest Held for Manslaughter, Six Negroes Indicted for Rape," *Coshocton
    Tribune* (Coshocton, Ohio), September 13, 1940, page 1.

"Woman Enters Innocent Plea in Double Slaying," *Martins Ferry Times
    Leader,* March 25, 1968, page 1.

"Woman Held for Deaths of Barnesville Couple," *Martins Ferry Times
    Leader,* March 23, 1968, page 1.